LAUNDRY WISDOM

Instructions for a Greener and Cleaner Life

Carin Froehlich

iUniverse, Inc.
New York   Bloomington

Laundry Wisdom
Instructions for a Greener and Cleaner Life

iUniverse books may be ordered through booksellers or by contacting:

iUniverse
1663 Liberty Drive
Bloomington, IN 47403
www.iuniverse.com
1-800-Authors (1-800-288-4677)

ISBN: 978-1-4401-9802-1 (sc)
ISBN: 978-1-4401-9800-7 (dj)
ISBN: 978-1-4401-9801-4 (ebk)

Library of Congress Control Number: 2009913374

Printed in the United States of America

iUniverse rev. date: 1/19/2010

DEDICATION

This book is lovingly dedicated to my grandchildren, Ava Noir and Mordecai Emmanuel, and to all of your grandchildren, whether they are here or yet to be.

CONTENTS

Acknowledgments ix

Preface xi

Chapter 1: Why Today? Why Now? 1
    The Good Old Days 5
    No Time, No Space, and Not Allowed 9
    The Right to Dry 9
    Bad Neighbors 10

Chapter 2: Mom's Advice 13
    Time Management 15
    Laundry Baskets or Hampers 16
    Clothes Hangers 17
    Drying Racks 18
    Laundry Rooms 18
    Laundromat 19
    Sorting Secrets 20
    Water Temperatures and the Cold Water Debate 21
    Removing Stains the Old-fashioned Way 22
    Travel Kit Stain Remover 23
    Shake It Out 23
    Soaking Clothes 23
    Hand Washing 24
    Static Cling 24
    Salt 25
    Dryer Balls 26

Chapter 3: Going Green 27
    Green History 29
    Laundry Detergents 31
    The Dryer Versus Hanging Your Clothes on the Line 33
    How to Install an Outdoor Clothesline 34
    Clothespins 35
    The Changes You Need to Make 35
    Laundry Stain Removers 40
    Allergies 41

Chapter 4: All About High-Efficiency Washers and Dryers 45
Types of HE Washers 47
Space 48
Color of the machine 48
Mold in HE Washers 50
Chlorine treatment 52
Baking Soda and Vinegar Treatment 53
Commercial Cleaners 54

Chapter 5: Exercise the Body and Mind 55

Chapter 6: Teach Your Children from Toddler to Teen 63
Teaching Green 65
Laundry Steps 67
Going Off to College: Laundry Instructions 70

Chapter 7: Make Your Own Laundry Products 75
Make Your Own Dryer Sheets 78
Make Your Own Spot Remover 78
Homemade Recipes 80
Mending Clothes 82
How to Sew on a Button 83
How to Sew a Hem 84

Chapter 8: The Joy of Laundry 85
The American Experience 87
"The Clothesline" by Marlyn K. Walker 87
"The Basic Rules for Clotheslines" by Lois Hermann 89
"Mom's Little Helper" by Joyce Murphy 90
"Laundry Memory" by Bonnie Halko 90
"Laundry in Bristol, Pennsylvania" by Kate Grow 91
"Mom's New-Fangled Clothes Pole" by Trudi Rosencrans 91
"Big Stinky" by Lane McLeish 92
"True Story" by Beverly Phillips 94
"Laundry Stories" by Cathryn Brownstein 94
"The Mystery of the Missing Socks" by Carin Froehlich 99
"Clothesline Harmony or the Wedding Catcher" by Anonymous . . 100
"Camping Laundry" by Sally Whiteson 101
"Grandma's Queenie 2 Trip" by Barbra Williams 102
"Laundromat, New York City, 1968" by Annie Percichello 103
"Wash Day" by Lidia Welks 104

A Note to the Reader 107

Acknowledgments

Thank you to all of the people who have helped me while I was writing *Laundry Wisdom*.

To my family, who experienced two years of laundry experiments; who ate whatever I prepared for meals, with no complaints. At all times, they tried to be courteous while I wrote. I am grateful.

To my friends (at least, I think they still are), who helped me with my "experiments" and listened patiently to all my laundry facts.

To Jane Lusaka and Cathy Redmond my editors (IUniverse) that spent countless hours on this book. Their dedication and magic has made my manuscript enjoyable.

To the staff at Staples for helping me cope with my limited knowledge of laptops. On July 31, 2009, they held my hand and gave me hugs after my computer crashed. My book was one chapter from completion.

To Alex Lee executive director, Project Laundry List,

To Derek and Lynn Reid, for listening to and helping me form my thoughts, and for allowing me to stay at their cottage while I wrote this book.

To my husband, Dietrich Emmanuel Froehlich, who ate a steady diet of salsa and chips, so I could keep on working. I am most grateful to God for you.

PREFACE

A perfect summer day is when the sun is shining, the breeze is blowing, the birds are singing, and the lawn mower is broken.
—James Dent

Laundry is an everyday experience for every soul who walks the earth. It doesn't matter who you are or what you do, or whether you are rich or poor—you have laundry. From the moment you are born until your last breath, you produce laundry. Washing clothes is a chore that has existed for thousands and thousands of years and never has a day off. As your life changes, so does your laundry. It can be a horror, or it can be a joy. I have spent years "accumulating" other people's memories of their laundry days. Many lessons can be learned from other people's stories. I also have researched every book and article on the topic that I could find, finally coming to the conclusion that there is no right or wrong way to do your laundry. Laundry is truly something you either hate or love. I have been on both sides of the line.

Over the years, I have developed entertaining and heartwarming comments and stories that I hope will inspire you to take a different view of laundry. I have created step-by-step instructions that will lead you to your own ritual of laundry care.

The recent economic crisis has touched every single family in America in one way or another. We all are scrambling for ways to reduce expenses, including those related to laundry, one of the largest consumers of energy in the home. This year, as millions of Americans look at their utility bills in horror, they're realizing that the time has come to stop living like their neighbors and to start looking at how their grandparents lived. It is not just the economy that is hurting; our natural supplies also are running low. Suddenly, we have come to the end of our so-called never-ending resources, and what we thought would always be there for us will not be. Consumption of energy must decrease in every household in America. It is time for every one of us, from every walk of life, to make the necessary changes in our everyday life style. It is no longer just a choice; it is mandatory.

In this book—and on my website, www.laundrywisdom. com—I point out many energy-saving ways to help families cut back. Occasionally using cold water or hanging laundry (indoors or outdoors) will lead to a difference in monthly electric or gas bills. I am a strong believer in climate change, and it seems to me everywhere you look today you see the word "green," but no clear explanations of what that means. I explore the meaning of green, the fads and the facts, so you can easily make your own decisions about what to do. This book is filled with tips and stories that I truly hope will give you and your family a new perspective on that never-ending chore called laundry. At the end of this book there is a section where you can write your own laundry story, to share with your family for generations to come.

Chapter One

Why Today? Why Now?

It was a hot day for October. The older I get, the more I seem to dislike the heat. Of course, I was rushing off to work. I was trying to multitask with half of my brain operating. It was the usual morning of phone calls, which always makes me late. I am a volunteer hospice nurse but only for friends and family. Every once in a while, I get a desperate phone call from a friend of a friend; on this morning, the call came from Gail and Jack. I never did figure out which friend of mine led them to me. I just let the wind carry me to Gail and Jack. They lived close by in a new development of row homes. Jack was a quiet, elderly man in the fourth stage of cancer. Gail was an extremely friendly soul. She was so glad to see me. We made the usual introductions, and I began to work. I started by reviewing Jack's case study. He had recently retired and, sadly, he'd gone to his family doctor for a routine check-up before he and Gail were to leave on their dream trip across the United States, a trip they would never take.

Jack was a man of few words. I am usually good at small talk, but with Jack, all I got was silence. At times, I felt as though I were intruding on his privacy. One day, I asked Jack in passing who was in the picture next to his bed. He answered, "My mother, Mary Mulligan, and what a great mother she was." I responded, "What a beautiful woman." Little by little Jack would drop me a clue about his mom. I boldly asked him, one day, "Do you think you'll get to see her soon?" He answered with a huge smile, "You betcha, kid!" For some reason, that day I had extra time to spare. I sat down next to him and agreed that, no doubt, she would be waiting for him. I asked him what he remembered most about his mother. He started telling me about how happy she would be on wash day. "Oh, the smell of fresh clean laundry." It surprised me because I was sure he would mention a favorite family recipe. "Laundry?" I asked. "How the hell could she have been happy with laundry? I need to know the secret!" He chuckled and stated that when he returned from the Korean War, as soon as he saw laundry hanging in the backyard, he knew he was home. Years later, when Jack and Gail got married, Gail said that they weren't even out of the church, and her mother-in-law was giving her laundry tips.

It is not part of my job to do laundry for my patients; in fact, the last time I checked, the hospice manual stated that it was forbidden. But I had this urge. Gail had gone shopping. I had some time. I sat Jack in his chair and stripped his bed. I found the laundry, put it in the washing machine, and off I went. The buzzer rang, and I returned. I marched outside and, to my surprise, there was no clothesline. In fact, when I looked around at the other houses, there was not a single clothesline in sight. "People are just too busy today," I thought to myself. I went up to the deck and hung the wet sheets over the rails and the pillow cases on the back of chairs. I was so proud of my makeshift line. It was a perfect fall day; the sun was out, the humidity was low, and the leaves were just starting to change. In no time, the sheets were dry, and I could put Jack back to bed.

The look on his face was worth a million dollars; he just couldn't believe I did that for him. "There is nothing," he said, "like the smell of clean sheets." I was running late and didn't even mention it to Gail. The next three times out, I did the same thing: I put the sheets in the washer before I did anything else and then took the wet laundry to the deck to dry. Jack was always glad to see me, and I felt that this simple chore broke the silence. I found it much easier to talk to him about dying, always telling him that his mom was right around the corner. Jack died on November 4, two hours after I had changed his sheets. It was a beautiful day; the sun was shining, and the leaves were at their peak. Fall had come pretty late that year.

I said my good-byes to the family. A few days later, I received a phone call from Gail, who gave me the funeral arrangements. I did not tell her, but I never attend the funerals of my patients. Because I have other patients and my own family to care for, I never seem to have enough time. In any case, the greatest gift I could give them was to be there at the time they needed me most. I believe that the funeral is the time when family and close friends should grieve.

I woke up on November 7; it was raining, and the plans I'd made had been cancelled. I started to do my laundry and thought, "I really should go to Jack's funeral." I entered the church, feeling nervous to be there by myself. As soon as I saw the beautiful flowers, the stunning stained-glass windows, and Jack's casket, I knew I had made the right decision. Later, back at Gail and Jack's house, many people approached me and thanked me for the great job I had done. Gail's sister commented, "Oh! He loved those sheets! It's a shame it cost them $150 in fines." I could not believe what I was hearing. Gail came up and put her arms around me and said, "We were never going to tell you. It was worth every cent. Jack so loved the smell and comfort of clean fresh laundry." I still could not understand what they were talking about. Gail's sister took me aside and explained that they were not allowed to hang out their laundry. I had broken the house association laws and caused a stir in the neighborhood. The association claimed that it received more than seventeen calls in one day. I could not believe it. I was truly horrified. I went home that day, and researched "home owners associations" online. I learned that while every one of them is different, they all have a specific set of often arbitrary rules that affect everything from roof repair to trash collection to clotheslines. My life changed forever. I started searching for Mary Mulligan's laundry secrets, determined to show that the "right to dry" belongs to all.

The Good Old Days

The goal in life is living in agreement with nature.
—Zeno of Citium (circa 355–circa 263 BCE)

Laundry is an everyday nightmare. It is a job that is never complete. "If only my family understood that," I mutter to myself as I put the last piece of laundry away. Almost immediately, it seems, there will be a wet towel in the laundry basket; two seconds later, here comes a dirty shirt. It never ever ends. I have spent the last two years studying and researching laundry, and the one word that keeps coming up is "organization." How do you organize the timing of dirty laundry? The only solution I have come up with is to make family members wear dirty clothes for five out of seven days.

My mother is the saint of laundry. She is from the old school, and I believe there was a dinosaur or two left in the world when she started washing clothes. Mom owns a dryer, but every Monday you can see her laundry hanging outside in perfect order. Mom is eighty years young, and it does not matter what the weather is, that she only has one leg that works, if she has the flu—it does not matter, her laundry gets done. My earliest memories are of doing laundry in Roslyn, Pennsylvania during the 1950s. We lived on Sixth Street. It was a working-class neighborhood in those days. Clotheslines were everywhere. My mom says that everyone hung their clothes on a line, even though everyone had a dryer. Laundry day was only on one day a week, and that day was Monday. After the weekend, there were enough leftovers from Sunday's dinner to feed everyone on Monday, which gave people enough time to finish the laundry task. The children who were not in school helped separate the clothes into three piles: whites, mediums, and darks. We washed the heaviest fabrics first, usually the darks, consisting of jeans and more jeans. The whites were last. Each piece of clothing was examined for mending and stains before it entered the washer. The whites and stained items were presoaked in hot-water tubs. The most important thing was to do the laundry from start to finish. There was no talking on the phone unless it was a true emergency.

Marion Sherman, who is ninety, lived in northeast Philadelphia, and she tells a different tale. She had to share her clothesline with the neighbor across the street, Mrs. Fisher. There were wheels attached to the second floors of their homes. The line stretched across the street to her neighbor's home and worked on a pulley system. Marion states that neighbors could use the line on different days of the week. The only time there was a problem was when the holidays arrived. Everyone wanted her tablecloth fresh off the line. When the skies clouded up and the first drops of rain fell, you could hear for miles, "Mrs. Fisher, it's going to rain!" No matter how well we knew our neighbors, we always addressed them by their last names. Marion was Mary Kirby's neighbor for some thirty years. But when they were on the street, it was never "Mary," it was Mrs. Kirby. If someone had a job, and it started to rain, neighbors that were home took down the laundry. It was never a problem; that was the way it was. In the 1960s, more and more women went back to work. They kept the same laundry schedule. This fact always amazed me—the communities not only helped each other, they teamed up to get the laundry done.

All the stories sound the same when it comes to gossip. (My mother corrects me when I say "gossip." She says, "It was not gossip, it was news. We didn't have all of this twenty-four-hour, seven-day weekly news cycle you have now.") People knew what was happening in the neighborhood by looking at what type of laundry was hanging outside. When someone was ill, the sheets would be plenty, and there would be extra wash. When a woman gave birth, she would hang pink or blue booties to let everyone know that she had a boy or a girl; other details about the birth would come from conversations over the fence. Whoever was in need got a casserole for dinner every night. This also was decided by the clothesline. Not much escaped these clothesline ladies, especially stains. They had Superman's eyes when it came to examining each other's wash. There would be such statements as, "I will have to let Mrs. Hutchison know that hydrogen peroxide will get that nasty stain out of Johnny's shirt.

When my children were young, I hung their diapers up twice a week. I seemed to be the only mother on the street who did so. I was amazed at what the women of the neighborhood would tell me: for example, "My daughter was potty trained at sixteen months." I would go into my house muttering, "Yeah, right! How can that be?" They all claimed that their children were potty trained by the time they were sixteen months of age. It wasn't until recently that one of them finally broke the code of silence and confessed, "Oh, honey, they didn't hang their diapers outside; they hung them in their basements!"

The clothesline had other purposes. If you had a secret you wanted to tell, you met your friend at the clothesline. My dad took the line down for summer picnics and hung the badminton net on the clothesline poles. My neighbor hung his fish on the clothesline. My in-laws hung chickens on the clothesline to drain and clean them. That was one of those jobs no one wanted to do, but it was all worth it when you sat down for that Sunday feast of roast chicken. One woman told me that she'd gotten her first kiss at the clothesline. I asked her "What happened to the front door?" She laughed and replied, "Everyone had their eye on the front door; back at the clothesline, nobody ever watched after 5 PM." Oh, really? I wonder if that would have worked in my neighborhood.

The grass always looks greener on the other side, but you still have to mow it!

Today, some products at my local grocer cost three times more than they did a year ago. Our electric bill has doubled in the last eight months. In addition, no one is looking forward to the deregulation that will characterize the future. Over the next few years the way we distribute and consume energy in the United States will change dramatically. Each state, if it has not already, will allow consumers to choose an electric company. Such deregulation often leads to higher prices for most and lower prices for very few. This is because a price-controlled system (what you have now) always undercharges. As a result, some claim that everyone's energy bills will increase 40 to 60 percent. Oh, joy! The clothesline gets better looking by the day. The clothes dryer is the second-largest consumer of electricity in the home. It is also the number one cause of house fires. In good weather, I hang my clothes outside, and in bad weather, I hang them indoors. I do laundry for five people, and I save over $86 a month on our electric bill. Using cold water and biodegradable soap that is reasonably priced saves money. I also have made my own detergent (look for the recipes later in this book). Making sure there is a full load every time you use the washer is another money-saving tip. Children often change their clothes frequently or try something on, decide they don't want to wear it, then take it off, and throw it on the floor in a ball. My two nieces, ages eleven and fourteen, are champions at this game. After I visited my sister a few times, we eliminated over 35 percent of her dirty laundry. Of course, both girls screamed at me, telling me that I was gross to put away something they'd had on their bodies for less than thirty-seven seconds (and after they had just taken their second shower of the day!). I just let them know that, for a change of pace, I could give them a haircut instead; you should have seen them run!

The recession may be making the United States a little smellier, the May 2009 *Pittsburgh Post-Gazette* reported. Americans are scrimping on laundry by buying cheaper detergent and dry-cleaning less often. According to one recent poll, 60 percent of shoppers wear their clothes multiple times between washings to save money (www. bureauoflaborstatistics.gov, 2008).

No Time, No Space, and Not Allowed

The Bureau of Labor Statistics states that the average American aged fifteen or older spends 108 minutes doing daily "household activities." This includes housework, cleaning, financial management, and laundry. The biggest complaint I hear, time and time again, is "I do not have the time." We have lost an awful lot of organizational tools in recent decades since the rise of new technologies. Ironically, these technologies were made to save us time and be more convenient. But how much time are we really saving, and what is the cost?

The Right to Dry

The Right to Dry movement arose because in many areas, people are not allowed to hang their laundry outside. Hundreds of thousands of home owner associations across America forbid residents to hang clotheslines. A lot of urban legends are associated with the clothesline, including the belief that it shows poverty and depletes property value by 15 percent. This is false. I have interviewed several hundred realtors across the country about this issue. Every one of them claimed that hanging laundry outside has never had an effect on property value. Another complaint is, "It ruins my view of nature." I find it hard not to reply, "Well, it is nature working for you." Ben Davis of www.right2dry. org once said, "It is hard for me to believe that you can have a AK-47 gun in your bedroom and [can] wake up tomorrow and start any type of religion you can think of, but you cannot hang a clothesline." Many states, including Vermont and Florida, have stepped up and changed the laws. Yet, there are a lot of places where the wonderfully drying American sun could do free of charge what otherwise takes a lot of energy and adds plenty to home owners' gas or electric bills. The sun requires no government subsidy, no tax rebate, and no expensive installation. On a hot day, the clothesline will dry clothes faster than an electric or gas dryer. As my husband says, "If we are to seriously take a look at alternative energy, we must seriously put an end to … local laws [denying people their] property rights." Tons of government money is being spent on windmills and solar panels; where will the government put them if people are not allowed to hang a clothesline? There are a lot of programs available online; just search for "right to dry." There is a wonderful documentary titled *Drying for Freedom* by Steven Lake, a native of England.

Bad Neighbors

Bad neighbors exist everywhere, and when it comes to hanging clotheslines, they rank right up there with "loud music and barking dogs." I believe that the bad-neighbor syndrome is the number one reason you do not see clotheslines throughout this country. Compared to the rest of the world, Americans are incredibly wealthy, which often creates a personal sense of entitlement. Some people think that our economic status entitles us to waste energy. We are just so special, our time is so important, we can waste all the energy we want. We actually look down on people who want to save the planet.

Our neighbors' opinions and priorities become more important to us than our own individual rights for freedom. These people will not even tolerate an open discussion on saving fossil fuels or global warming; they label anyone who does a hippie or a left-wing idiot. I had one discussion with an environmental attorney who listened patiently to my complaints about trying to hang a clothesline and dealing with unfriendly neighbors who put nasty letters in my mailbox. He finally said, "Let me get this straight. Who is the bad neighbor and who is the good neighbor?" Well, of course, I was the good neighbor. He replied, "Oh, no! You're both wrong! Did you ever ask them if it was alright to hang a clothesline?" I replied, "No!"

"Well, maybe you should approach them with your thoughts on green savings in a positive way and an upbeat manner," he said. "If they still disagree, don't hang the clothesline! Remember there are two sides of the street called diversity. A happy neighborhood is far more important than angering your neighbor by hanging a line!"

Needless to say, I did not ever call him back. He had a point, though: world peace or a clothesline. The Internet is full of advice about bad neighbors. Brant Walker runs rotten neighbor.com(under construction), and he has the best solutions on the Internet. Brant's says there are two sides to every story. Of course, both sides are right. The real secret is trying to get neighbors to appreciate each other's views. Know your neighbors. Knock on their doors. I recently decided to take Mr. Walker's advice, and it worked out splendidly. I took my neighbors a list of why I wanted to hang out my clothes and they pleasantly agreed. Of course, they are not running out and putting up their own clotheslines. But they agreed to respect my values, and that is more than enough for me. In addition, it turned out that the letters in my mailbox were not written by my immediate neighbors but by someone who drives around "spreading hate."

CHAPTER TWO

MOM'S ADVICE

One generation plants the trees; another gets the shade.
—Chinese proverb

I have collected hundreds of laundry tips and ideas from across the country. I was recently reminded by a gentleman that it is not just moms who do laundry. He has been doing the laundry for his family for the last thirty-one years and also works full time as a doctor. I soon found out that a lot of fathers do the laundry. (I have brought this fact up to my husband, but he pretends he can't hear me. Perhaps some of you will have better luck with your own spouses.) There are so many different ways of organizing laundry. I have been overwhelmed with tips, and they all are excellent. I have divided them into subjects to make for easier reading. Not all them will apply to everyone's lifestyles; pick and choose what is best for you. Make your own plan.

Time Management

Time and organization seem to be the first items on everyone's laundry list; a lot of these hints will aid in both of these areas. If you feel overwhelmed, overworked, that no way, no how can you accomplish what needs to be done, take a deep breath, and chalk it up to heredity. It is a matter of mind and not just time management. If I have to do anything that I feel is boring, I begin to come up with excuses for why I should not do it right away. The laundry gets put off for a time, but the next day, the loads are larger. The best advice I can give you is that it will not go away. Getting the family to help more may seem hard to do, but once you make steadfast rules and stick to them, it begins to go a whole lot better. Once rules become habit, you are on your way. It is like going on a laundry diet. You can do it! The following is a collection of organizational tips that may help you establish your own personal laundry ritual.

Laundry Baskets or Hampers

Put a basket for collecting dirty laundry in each person's bedroom. Set up different baskets for different types of clothes. If you have the space, use three hampers—one for whites, one for towels, and one for darks. The rules are as follows:

- Every article must be turned right-side-out.
- No wet or damp wash, may be put into any hamper.
- Use a separate laundry basket for soiled or stained items.
- Keep an extra spray bottle or pre-treating stick in your dirty clothes basket so you can deal with stains immediately.
- Keep two extra baskets by your dryer, which always helps when you have extra laundry.
- Sort clothes in tall kitchen garbage pails, plastic milk crates, large buckets, or any other item you can recycle.
- Small baskets available at dollar stores make perfect infant and baby laundry baskets.

Use a different laundry basket for each member of the family. I tried to give baskets of different colors to each of my family members but quickly found out that baskets come in only three colors. So I decided to have the same size basket for everyone; they are just of different shapes. My family of five does not separate their clothes, however; I do that in the laundry room. I take everyone's basket out to the clothesline. I fold the clothes right after I take them from the line or the dryer and put them in the basket. It has saved me a lot of time.

Smaller laundry baskets are a great idea for smaller children. Even though only a few clothes may fit in a small container, some claim the process has taught their toddlers the responsibility of taking their clothes to their rooms. Keep a small basket next to your washer and dryer for mismatched socks and another one somewhere in the laundry room for clothes that need mending. If your house has a laundry chute, put a basket on a skateboard directly below it. When you are ready to do laundry, simply roll the load to the washer. Use white laundry baskets for whites, and colored laundry baskets for colors. Don't throw everything into the laundry basket right away. If an item gets a stain, take a damp, soapy sponge and scrub it out; then put the item somewhere to dry. Never leave clean laundry unfolded in the basket. Everything should go straight from the dryer or clothesline to the closet or drawers. Postponing the tasks of folding and putting the clothes away makes laundry twice as hard.

Clothes Hangers

Hang clothes as soon as they are removed from the dryer. I like to use the cheap wire hangers, because I can twist the hook any which way and hang it anywhere. I have read articles that state that wire hangers cause rust. I have never seen a speck of rust on any of my clothes. If you fear rust, however, buy hangers with swivel hooks, which usually are made from plastic. I recently found wooden swivel hangers at the dollar store; they are absolutely the best.

Always shake the item before you hang it up. Secure shirts by buttoning the first two or three buttons before hanging them in the closet. Make sure to leave half an inch between items, so they won't wrinkle. Put items on hangers as soon as you take them from the washer. Then put the hanger right on to the clothesline. If it is windy, use a clothespin to secure the hanger. When the clothes are dry, take the hanger right to the closet. When drying clothes inside, put the hanger on the shower rod. Leave an inch or two for circulation.

One person told me that she never uses a dryer anymore; she takes everything out of the washing machine and puts it onto hangers in the closet, leaving three inches between items as they dry. She also noted she had lots of closet space. A college student cut his laundry in half by hanging his worn but unstained clothes onto a hanger at the end of every day. Of course, socks and unmentionables (underwear) always went to the laundry basket. His whole dorm adopted this practice and also demanded that the administration put drying racks in the laundry room.

Drying Racks

My grandmother had a wooden drying rack, and she would dry her unmentionables indoors on the rack instead of outside on the line. Racks are becoming popular once again. Drying clothes indoors adds humidity to the air, which is very much needed in the winter time. People with little or no space have found very creative ways to use these racks to dry their clothes. My friends, Ruth and Gregg Heath actually hang a retractable line in their living room. They live in NH, and when the weather does not permit them to go out they hang their clothes inside. There are many great places to buy these racks and lines.

Laundry Rooms

Many spaces in a home today can be designated as laundry areas. The basement seems to be the most popular, especially in older homes. The basement is the farthest place you can go, but the cheapest to set up with plumbing. If you are fortunate to have a basement that you can stand up in, you have the space for a laundry room. My sister's laundry room is on the second floor, which makes it close to the dirty laundry, although it is cramped for space. She hangs the wet clothes outdoors so she still has to clump up and down the steps. Some folks have laundry rooms in their garages, and some even have set them up in an outside shed. We could never entertain that because we lived in a cold climate, and the pipes would freeze.

Organizing these areas, wherever they may be, is a must. Depending on the space, some of these ideas will not work. Install or utilize existing Shelving for your detergent, bleach, and fabric softeners. Baskets in all sizes, perfect for organizing dirty laundry, are available from the dollar store. To find the basket that is appropriate for your space, first, choose some laundry supplies that are close in size to the ones you use. Wheel them over to the basket aisle and place the supplies in various baskets, picking the shapes and sizes that work. Wheel the supplies back to where you found them, and head home with your new baskets—storage containers for your laundry supplies. Use an over-the-sink basket to hold detergents. Set up the laundry area for efficiency. A good lighting system will help you see stains better. A rack will allow you to hang clothes as soon as you take them from the dryer; a cheap shower tension rod is great for hanging clothes. A folding space is very important; some people use their couch and fold as they watch TV. A folding TV tray by the dryer works just as well. Make sure the laundry basket is secure on the table before you start. This will prevent a lot of unnecessary bending.

Laundromat

Commercial washers and dryers are more efficient than domestic versions, so taking your clothes to the Laundromat is a way to use less energy. There is a Laundromat in our town that heats water with solar energy. Here are a few tips for making the best use of your time. Before you go to the Laundromat, separate your clothes into white, darks, and delicates. Check for stains and clothes that need mending. Check all the pockets for nonwashable items, such as coins and lipstick, etc.

Treat stained items with a stain remover. If the garment is new and may bleed, hand wash it at home, and dry it with the dark-color clothes at the Laundromat. Soak clothes that need it in a sink or pail; rinse in the tub and wring them out. Then snap the items, and fold them wet into the laundry basket. At the Laundromat, place them into dryer with the other wet clothes.

Sort the laundry, and bundle each load with a belt to make it easier to carry it to the Laundromat. Instead of lugging that big bottle of laundry detergent around, place some of the detergent in an old mayonnaise jar or another container with a tight-fitting lid. If you use powdered detergent, use a ziplock baggie. Do the same with your other laundry supplies. When you are done, place all of the products into a small basket.

Put quarters into empty film canisters. Or rinse out a small, used detergent container several times, dry it, and use it to collect change all week long at home. Replace the cap, and take the container with you to Laundromat. It makes a cool change purse because it has a handle and makes it easier to put coins in machines. Keep a small bag filled with extra-large garbage bags in your car at all times. If it rains, you can put your finished laundry into the bags. After you put the laundry away, recycle the garbage bags by placing them back in the smaller bag and into the car.

At the Laundromat, make use of the double- or triple-load washers; if you have more than one load of clothes, this will save energy. Bring reading material with you to pass the time. Start the machines at different intervals so that not everything is done at once. Always check the washer or dryer before you use it. The person who used the machine before you may have left some items behind, or you might have an experience like one that I am still trying to recover from, even though it happened over twenty years ago. It was the one time that I was in a rush and did not check the dryer. I cleaned the lint trap and piled in my laundry. Of course, the load included some of my favorite clothes. I slammed the lid down and added my quarters. I heard a racket but thought that the machine had a loose part, so I did not go back to check it. When the buzzer went off, I ran to open the lid and saw a rainbow of florescent purple. I could not figure out what it was, but then I saw an empty nail-polish bottle. I could not believe the contents of such a tiny bottle could spread so far. For about two weeks, I tried every stain remover I could dream of, finally giving up and throwing all of the clothes away. Oh, yes, there were tears in my eyes!

Sorting Secrets

Sorting clothes is one laundry chore you just can't skip. Once I went to my son's first apartment, where I was greeted by one hundred empty pizza boxes. He and his roommate had worked very hard to accumulate that many boxes. The next shock was the "laundry baskets," in which clean and dirty clothes were mixed together. It never had dawned on me to tell my son never to mix his clean and dirty laundry. I started to separate it when I noticed that everything smelled moldy and had a pink tint to it. My son started to explain. "Mom, I save so much time throwing all the laundry in together at once." In the end, however, I lucked out. He started dating a wonderful girl, who did all of his laundry and turned out to be the best daughter-in-law a parent could ask for.

Sorting laundry can be time-consuming, but it is well worth the effort. You will save time and energy and end up with laundry loads that look clean and smell fresh. As you start to sort, remember to empty all pockets, and close zippers to prevent sagging. Check for stains and heavily soiled items. Separate the heavily soiled items from the lightly soiled ones since the lightly soiled clothes will pick up the extra dirt from the wash water. Whites will come out grayer or dingy; colors will become duller and duller. Separate by color. Put all of the whites in one pile, all the lights in another, and the bright and dark colors in a third pile. Then check the color pile for noncolorfast items, i.e., any article of clothing that could bleed into the rest of the wash load. Combine the piles. Once you have sorted, the trick is to combine the different piles into like groups; put whites and light-colored articles with similar amounts of soil into one group; separate the colors and add gray articles to this pile. I soak all of my heavily soiled items first and then add them wet to these piles. It sounds ridiculous, but it really saves time and will come to you naturally after you perform this task a few times. One big time-saver is to make sure that everyone puts his or her dirty laundry into the hamper right-side out. It is a nightmare to straighten out balls of dirty clothes. I have seen people (whose names I will not mention) who stick the laundry into the washer machine like this. They also take the laundry from the washer to the dryer in a ball. I guarantee that those items will not come out clean. In addition, the items take twice as long to dry and have a ton of wrinkles.

Watch out for lint. Keep fabrics that produce lint, like towels, separate from fabrics that attract lint, like sweaters and corduroys. I never mix my towels or terry-cloth items with any other laundry. One of the top reasons sheets get those annoying nips is from mixing towels with cotton. Avoid separating your piles into loads that are too small or too large. Washing machines should never be more than three-quarters full. Loads of clothes that are too small are not more efficient either; instead, you waste water and electricity. If you have one or two items, either wash by hand, or wait till you can acquire a larger load.

Water Temperatures and the Cold Water Debate

One of the biggest ways to save on the cost of laundry is to use cold water. Many articles have been written on this subject. Using cold water for all of your wash will make a huge difference in your electric or gas bill. Cold water is recommended to be safe for washing all fabrics. The old standard rules were always to use hot water for your whites, heavily stained or soiled clothes, or greasy stains. Warm water was suggested for permanent press and any other 100-percent manmade fibers and moderately soiled items. Cold water was used the first time new items were washed because it would keep most dyes in dark or bright-colored clothing from bleeding and all clothes from shrinking. Cold water also is good for certain types of stains, such as blood, wine, grape juice, or coffee. I use cold water for *some* of my wash loads. I cannot be a hero and use it every time. When I worked at a local emergency department, where I encountered different infections on a daily bases, I had to use hot water. My husband farmed, my sons did auto repair; I used hot water. When family members are sick with one thing or another, I use hot water. Greasy stains are impossible to remove with cold water. I have seen many new detergents on the market that claim to work best in cold water. I have experimented with these products and found only one difference from other types of detergents: they dissolved too quickly in water and were worse at removing dirt.

Removing Stains the Old-fashioned Way

When you stop to think about it, wash is nothing but stains. There are a million stains and a million products on the market to help you get rid of them. Then there is good old grandma's way of removing stains. They all work; the difference is just a matter of how much time you want to spend on laundry and how environmentally safe you would like to be. My mom always kept a chart in her washing room with a list of stain-removal ideas. As the years went on, she would amend that list, cross off one idea, and add another. Today, that list could be a book all of its own. I can never read it without being totally amazed about the various ways there are to remove a stain. My mom reminds me that laundry used to be a huge topic of conversation at parties. The men would sit in one room and tell dirty jokes, and the women would sit in another room and talk about great recipes and stain removal. Until recently, I cannot remember having a stain-removal conversation with my friends. Now that I am writing this book, of course, I get emails and phone calls: "Hey, Carin! How do you get spaghetti stains out again?" I take pride on being a stain guru. I keep a copy of my mom's list with me at all times. The list is on my website: www.laundrywisdom.com.

Travel Kit Stain Remover

Put together a travel stain kit, namely a small bottle with a pull-up lid. Fill it with your favorite detergent. I prefer Green Works by Clorox. The key to successful stain removal is to treat the stain before it sets or dries in your garment. My friend Kate made a travel stain kit for me when I went to visit my first grandchild. I keep it in my glove compartment. Honestly, I use it more for my husband and myself than for the grandkids. It is a nifty idea because you can refill the bottle easily. These kits also make great gifts for newlyweds or new moms.

Shake It Out

This term—shake it out—echoes in my ears every time I hang laundry. The idea is to shake, snap, or jerk every item of clothing taken out of the washer and then again when hanging it or putting it in a dryer. It is the number-one sure way to get rid of wrinkles and allow the clothing to dry properly. To be honest, I shake the clothes only before hanging or placing it in a dryer. My mom, the queen shaker, has caught me more than once over the years skimping on my shaking. I tell her that I am saving energy or preventing carpal tunnel in my wrists. Hanging your clothes on a clothesline rids all fabric of wrinkles. To prevent wrinkles on permanent press fabrics, wash and rinse in cold water; then place a dry towel with the wet clothes in the half-filled dryer. Do not forget to fold or hang the clothes as soon as the dryer or hanging is done.

Soaking Clothes

Soaking clothes in large tubs overnight used to be common in the old days. Today, you spray on commercial stain remover, and don't think twice. If the garment does not come clean, some people throw it away, believing that it will be impossible to get the stains out. This is sad because with simple things like salt, white vinegar, hydrogen peroxide, and a good soak, the stain will disappear. Fill a bucket or sink with warm to hot water, just enough to cover the garment completely. Before putting the garment in the sink or bucket, add a one-quarter cup of white vinegar or a one-quarter cup of washing soda to the water. Soak overnight. It takes no huge effort and works extremely well.

Hand Washing

Hand washing uses the same rules as those for soaking clothes except that there is an extra step: rinse out more than once. This method is great for delicates. Use a very small amount of detergent when washing by hand. The old steps for hand washing are as follows: first, fill the basin or sink with cool water. My Nana used ice-cold water; if your hands can stand this, go ahead. Add a capful of your favorite delicate-wash detergent. Woolite is mine. Swish the items, one or two at a time, gently through the suds. Soak for a few minutes. Then drain the basin or sink, and gently squeeze the sudsy water from the items. Rinse twice in a sink filled with clean water. Rinse a third time if you see suds after the second rinse. When washing smaller delicates, I sometimes run the item under the cold-water faucet to ensure a good rinse. Squeeze the items gently, and roll them in a clean white towel. Do not use a colored towel. I once used a beach towel, and the colors rolled right onto my delicates. Press the towel gently to remove as much water as you can. Hang on a hanger and hang in your shower or outside. All washers today offer a delicate cycle, but I still prefer Nana's way for my favorite items. To prevent your sweaters from pilling, place them in a pillowcase and tie it closed with string before placing it in the washing machine.

Static Cling

Triboelectric charging (a good Scrabble phrase), the technical name for static cling, occurs when two objects rub together and an electric charge builds up between them. If the electrical charge is released, it can cause a slight shock that is uncomfortable, but my children act as if it is deadly. If the electricity is not released, the objects may stick together. Fabric softeners reduce or eliminate static cling by adding a thin layer of a chemical lubricant to the clothing, either in the wash or through sheets in the dryer. When I started my research on fabric softeners, I was shocked to find that they all use beef tallow or fat of some kind. Whether scented or unscented, they lead to the same results. What a lot of people do not understand is that fabric softener enters your skin. It is now believed, based on some studies, to cause serious respiratory problems, especially in infants. It is stated right on most boxes and bottles that fabric softeners are not recommended for baby clothes because they eliminate the flame retardant on clothing. This is just one of the problems caused by fabric softeners. They are the number-one reason for dryer fires. Removing just the lint from the dryer is not enough; the fat or wax build-up also should be removed from the lint screen. It is amazing how much better the dryer works after the screen is cleaned with soap and hot water. My mother has never needed to use fabric softener; she adds a half cup of white vinegar to the washing machine, which does not smell like vinegar when the wash is done. Try it, if only once; please give it a try.

Salt

My mom adds a quarter cup of salt to the wash so her clothes will not freeze on the clothesline in the winter. I soak my wooden clothespins in two cups of salt dissolved in two cups of water. Bring to a boil, let cool, then hang the pins on the line to dry. I do this once a year, and my wooden pins never freeze in the winter. My mother adds a quarter-cup of salt every time she washes her towels, and it keeps them from getting stiff on the outdoor line. Some people like their towels stiff. I do not like it when they are so stiff you can stand them up in a corner by themselves. I have found that by adding two tablespoons of detergent, half a cup of white vinegar, and a quarter cup of salt to a full load of towels, I get perfect results. It sounds like a salad-dressing recipe; if I added oil, I could make fabric softener.

For those of you who just don't want to give up fabric softeners, try using half a sheet each time you use the dryer or half the amount you usually use in the washer. For those of you wondering what to do with a box of 250 dryer sheets, I have found that putting one in my vacuum bag works great. Every time I turn the vacuum on, I give out a clean, fresh scent. I have also found they are the best way to get rid of mice. We have an old home, and we have mice. My husband, the "great white hunter," loves to catch them in traps, but I am not fond of this whatsoever, especially in the morning when I open the cabinet and there one is. I had read that mice do not like it when you place dryer sheets in corners and have had great success with this. You do have to change the sheets once a month; when they lose their smell, the mice recycle them for their nests.

Dryer Balls

This is another gadget that works against static cling. These lightweight blue balls, roughly the size of baseballs, are sold in pairs. I have seen them in drugstores and some supermarkets. The balls have surface nodules that keep clothes fluffed in the dryer. These balls also dry your clothing faster, probably not twice as fast, but they do work. The only complaint I have is they are loud. When I close the laundry room door, however, I can't hear them bouncing around as much. My sister claims that tennis balls from the dollar store work just as well. I have tried using tennis balls, however, and think dryer balls work better. Make sure you do not confuse dryer balls and laundry balls, which are for the washer. Not only do they cost a lot, they did not work at all for me.

CHAPTER THREE

GOING GREEN

Bad habits are like a comfortable bed—easy to get into, but hard to get out of.

Green History

Today, everywhere you look, you can see and hear the word "green." I can't help but think of little green men every time I hear the word, probably due to the fact that I was born in the 1950s. What does it mean? The best definition that I could find was in an online blog, which stated that "green" refers to an individual action that a person can consciously take to stop harmful effects on the environment through consumer habits, behavior, and lifestyle.

The word green makes me think of something that is smart or wise. Green says fresh, clean, money. Many people think that living green is about making smart choices or that it is a holistic way of living. Others think that it is a joke, a smart way for corporations to make more money. Since there are no regulations at this time to determine what green is, it is up to consumers to educate themselves and their families and establish their own standards. Everywhere you look, there is green dining, green buildings, and green communities. I often wonder if green tea was the start of all this. When looking at ingredients in laundry detergents, you are better off looking at what they do not contain. Most manufacturers do not list what their products contain, and they are not yet required to by law because such information is considered a trade secret.

The green movement actually started hundreds of years ago. Green is an environmentalism movement to protect the quality and continuity of life through conservation of natural resources, prevention of pollution, and control of land use. The philosophical foundations for environmentalism in the United States were established by the separate efforts of Thomas Jefferson, Ralph Waldo Emerson, and Henry David Thoreau, among others. In 1864, George Perkins Marsh published *Man and Nature*, in which he anticipated many of today's ecological concepts. President Theodore Roosevelt was an early conservationist at a time when very few people were concerned about the environment. Supported by his friends, Gifford Pinchot, a leading advocate of environmental conservation who later became the first chief of the U. S. Forest Service, and John Muir, founder of the Sierra Club, Roosevelt stepped up to the plate. In 1906, he signed the American Antiquities Act, which helped organize the national parks. The Sierra Club, Audubon Society, the Izaak Walton League, and other environmental groups were established either just before or in the years following the turn of the twentieth century and are still active to this very day. But it wasn't until the 1950s and 1960s that the public at large became aware of the need to protect the endangered environment. People became very concerned about air and water pollution, trash disposal, dwindling energy resources, radiation, pesticide poisoning, and other environmental problems. They gave a huge push start to the new environmentalism.

In 1970, the first Earth Day, founded to encourage people to preserve the planet, opened the door even wider; it was soon followed by establishment of the Environmental Protection Agency (EPA). Thousands of new laws went into effect, focused on such things as pesticides, toxic substances, and ocean dumping. Federal agencies were required to file impact statements assessing the environmental consequences of proposed projects, ranging from dams and bridges to highways and airports to nuclear plants. These laws led to pollution research, which in turn led to the enactment of the 1980 Superfund Act, established to clean up toxic property in the United States, among other laws.

In the 1980s, however, during the terms of President Ronald Reagan and George H. W. Bush, many of the acts were allowed to expire, and environmental protection was practically brought to a standstill. In the early 2000s, the public started to see and feel the effects of global warming, although many claimed it was a huge joke.

Large corporations incorporated information about global warming into their marketing campaigns, which led to the green lifestyle for the better of mankind. Wal-Mart, the country's largest retailer, kicked off one of the largest green movements by determining the social and environmental impact of every item place on its shelves. The company has recently hired scholars, suppliers, and environmental groups to help create an electronic indexing system to rate every item—essentially, the green equivalent of nutritional labels. Wal-Mart claims that this technology will be completed in less than five years (between 2009 and 2014). Green lodging facilities is another growing trend. More hotels are looking for ways to become more environmentally friendly, which in turn is leading to increased requests from lodging properties for green laundry programs.

The words "natural" and "organic" have been associated with various products for years. Today, there are strict rules and regulations for using the word organic. Companies must be certified organic (i.e., their products are made without chemical additives) before they can even print it on their products. I have always been somewhat skeptical of organic foods. The cost is much higher, sometimes double the price for certain products. I have spent years working with specialty foods, knowing that certain companies were bottling spices that were definitely not organic and laughing all the way to the bank. Today, there are laws that somewhat guarantee that the product is indeed organic. There are no laws pertaining to the word "natural," however. The U.S. government does not regulate so-called natural products; anything can be labeled "natural," even products made of mostly synthetic ingredients. Many ingredients were given special exemptions when the Food, Drug, and Cosmetic Act was passed in 1938. As established by the act, the Food and Drug Administration (FDA) cannot order those products to be removed from the market even if they prove to be harmful.

Laundry Detergents

Laundry detergents and fabric softeners are now closely scrutinized by the public. While there used to be maybe one or two natural products in the supermarket, now there seems to be a new green product every week. People also have realized that many of these products have toxins that can be absorbed through the skin. In reality, nearly every chemical that touches the skin finds its way into the body and into the bloodstream. The skin is actually the largest organ in the body; it covers and protects everything inside. The skin is very important to a person's health and well being.

Families do not use household detergents just once in a while, however; they use them every day. When you wear clothes dried with dryer sheets or liquid fabric softeners, your body moisture causes those chemicals to come into contact with your skin and then to be absorbed directly into the bloodstream. Unscented products cause the same problems as scented ones do, particularly in infants. Research during the last two years (2006–2008) has linked asthma and respiratory problems in children under two years of age to detergents and fabric softeners.

The green way is to add half a cup of baking soda to the wash; this softens clothes naturally. Vinegar also works well to soften clothes. Add half a cup of white vinegar only to the wash, and presto—soft clothes. In fact, most of the cleaning comes from the water and the agitation of the machine and not from the detergent. There are products available on the market, but beware of scams. The biggest scam I fell for was the laundry balls known as ecoballs. These are not the same as the ones that you use in the dryer. These are made for the washer and are to be used instead of detergent. The manufacturer states that ecoballs wash your clothes by ionizing the water. That description should have raised a red flag. I paid $75 for mine, only to discover that they do absolutely nothing that plain water would not do. My friend, Joyce, whom I forced to buy and try them, called to say, "Turn on *Dateline*. They have a story about how bogus the laundry ball is. Thanks! You owe me $75!" Great, now I am down $150 for two useless balls.

Soap nuts are another substitute for detergent. They come from trees that grow in India and Nepal. They have a pleasant scent. I have found soap nuts to be effective but not inexpensive. They come with a little bag. I don't know what happened to my bag of soap nuts; maybe a squirrel came and stole it. Anyway, I made my own little soap nut bag, and the next thing I knew, my wash was loaded with these gritty little stones. Needless to say, I stuck the rest in my laundry drawer, and now their scent fills the drawer.

If you do use a detergent, always choose a biodegradable one; this is particularly important if your laundry water goes into a septic tank or similar wastewater treatment system. Organic detergents are biodegradable, and most contain plant oils and no petroleum, just like all the green detergents.

The Dryer Versus Hanging Your Clothes on the Line

Without a doubt, hanging your clothes on a line outdoors or inside your home beats using a dryer. How much energy does a clothes dryer use? Project Laundry List (www.laundrylist.org) has a calculator system that reveals exactly how much. A clothes dryer in operation uses about four kilowatts of power per hour or two kilowatt hours every thirty minutes.

In 1935, a man named J. Ross Moore built a dryer to spare his mother from having to hang wet laundry outside in the brutal North Dakota winter. Moore's patented dryers ran on either gas or electric power, but he was forced to sell the design to the Hamilton Manufacturing Company because he needed money. A clothes dryer is one of the most expensive appliances to operate; the longer it runs, the more money it costs. Dryer sheets can cause the dryer to work harder and end up costing even more money. On average, a full load of wet clothes contains about one gallon of water. As water is removed from the clothes, lint is created. The National Fire Protection Association (NFPA) estimates that fifteen thousand dryer fires occur each year. This translates into $67.7 million in direct property damage. Clothing is the most common source of ignition, followed by dust, fiber, and the aforementioned lint.

The clothesline causes far less trouble than the dryer. The clothesline works free of charge; in addition, there is documented proof that the sun and fresh air kill bacteria and disinfect faster than any chemical. (Some people prefer to turn their colored clothes inside-out, so they will not fade in the sun.) Watch your electric meter while your dryer is running. You will see with your own two eyes how quickly your money is sucked up by the electric company. It spins faster than the wheel of fortune. I could go on for a couple more pages, but instead I will give you instructions on how to hang up your new clothesline. If you already have and use one, you are my hero! Line drying achieves the scent that every detergent company is trying to capture.

How to Install an Outdoor Clothesline

First, find the spot that offers the most sun and space. It is okay if there is some shade. Sometimes people tie a line in between two trees. My sister Cindy does this; she actually moves her line to different areas of the yard depending on how much laundry she has for the day. If you have a porch, you can run the line from pole to pole. Look around and see what works best for you. One woman told me that she uses a retractable line on her front lawn, which works perfectly for her. The correct height of a clothesline will be different for everyone. My mom extended her arms above her head, and that was how high she put her line. Seven- to eight-feet high is the general rule. Determine what is best for you, but don't hang it too low, or the laundry will touch the ground. The length of the line should be anywhere between twenty and thirty-five feet. Then again, this is your line, and you know what you need best. You will need a screwdriver, drill, heavy-duty hook, metal eye hook, a cleat (a small metal wedge to wrap the rope around to anchor it), and a metal hook. If you cannot picture these items, ask for help at your local hardware store. Staff there also will be more than happy to show you manufactured clotheslines that come assembled. That decision is up to you. I splurged on a retractable clothesline, and I love it. You also need two strong supports; again, you can use trees or the columns of your porch. If you don't have these, you can buy poles just for clotheslines.

When you return from the hardware store, start by marking how high you want the line to be on each support. On one support, screw in the heavy-duty hook at the point you marked; start the hole with a drill. On the other support, screw in the eye hook. Twelve inches below the eye hook, install the cleat. Using a real tight knot, tie one end of the rope to the ring of the eye hook. Loop the ring over the first hook, and walk the rope (you can skip) over to the other support; thread the other end through the eye hook, pull it really tight again, and wrap it around the cleat to secure. Please e-mail me (see "A Note to the Reader") when you put up your first clothesline, or if you move and put up a new line. I have a thank-you gift for you.

Clothespins

Known in the United Kingdom and Ireland as clothes-pegs, clothespins have been reinvented countless times over the course of history. They are now a collector's item. In 1999, there was even an exhibit of clothespins at the Smithsonian Institution. It was spectacular, and I believe that you can still find information about it on the museum's website today. For a period of time, "clothespin art" was very popular. I can remember making Christmas decorations with clothespins as a kid. The clothespin originated with the Shaker movement in New Hampshire; the Shakers were the first to mass-produce them. The following story has been repeated for centuries: fishermen who were out at sea first designed the clothespin to hang their wash. The first pegs were sticks with a slit in the end, which was pushed over the garment to keep it on the line. The clothes-peg was patented in March 1832; it was described as a bent strip of hickory held together with a wooden screw, which proved to be totally impracticable. Rain or even dampness would cause the screw to swell, making the pin unusable. It took another twenty-one years for someone to come up with a design that would work in all climates. The "spring clamp" was invented in 1853 by David M. Smith of Springfield, Vermont—two wooden legs hinged together by a metal spring. It is the same clothespin design that we use today. That was followed by 146 other patents for clothespin in the mid-nineteenth century. Some people believe that the quest for the perfect clothespin (peg) has continued to this day.

The Changes You Need to Make

Here are a few suggestions and tips to help you do green laundry. You will save money and, at the same time, save the planet.

1. Wear it more than once. As I have mentioned earlier, if it isn't dirty, don't wash it! Do you wash your coat every time you wear it? I seriously hope the answer is no. Wearing your clothes more than once is the first big step to making your laundry green. According to the United

Nations Environmental Programme, you can consume up to five times less energy by wearing your jeans at least three times, washing them in cold water, and skipping the dryer or the iron. Use bath towels more than once. Always hang the towels on hooks to dry right after using them. Make sure you hang up clothes that can be worn again, so they are not washed by mistake.

2. Maximize your washer for energy efficiency. If you have a top-loader washing machine, chances are that you are using twice as much water per load than if you had a newer, front-loading machine. Front-loading washing machines (also known as horizontal axis washers) bearing the Energy Star logo use between eighteen and twenty-five gallons of water per load, while older machines use forty gallons per load. Whether or not you are ready to replace your washing machine, there are things you can do to increase its efficiency. Double-spin the clothes in the washer. After your washing machine is done, turn the knob to "spin only," and spin the clothes a second time. (If you hear water running, you have turned the knob to "rinse and spin." Use a sharpie and mark the area for spin only.) The centrifugal motion, i.e., the spinning, helps to get extra water out of the clothes, which means that they'll need less time in the dryer or on the clothesline.

3. Wash in cold water when applicable. Ninety percent of the energy used for washing clothes goes to heating the water, at a cost of hundreds of dollars each year. Soak heavily soiled items overnight; then wash them with lightly soiled clothes in cold water. Whites come out just as white with cold water. Cold-water temperatures also help preserve the fibers in fabric, meaning that they will not wear out as fast. With the exception of clothing made of wool, you cannot shrink a garment in cold water. But wool will shrink in water of any temperature. Go ahead and try using cold water, and tell me if you see a difference.

Wash only full loads, which will ensure that your machine is working at peak efficiency. There will be times when you cannot fill your washer to full capacity, so try this idea. Double-up your half loads of wet laundry and only dry full loads. Put your half load of washed whites in the dryer, but do not turn it on until your second half load has been washed. Dry both halves as one full load, and cut the energy costs in half. What if the second half load is composed of colors? Throw it in with the whites. The only exception here is if there is something new among the color load, and there is a possibility it will bleed. Hang it up to air dry before putting the rest of the color load in the dryer with the whites.

The Centers for Disease Control recommend that if you wash in cold water, you must use a dryer on the highest temperature allowed by the garment labels a minimum of twenty minutes or more. For example, when my kitchen rag starts to smell, I wash it in hot water and line dry it. If someone has the flu in your household, wash their clothes in hot water and put them in the dryer for at least twenty minutes. What many people do not understand about bacteria or germs is that they can easily spread from one laundry item to another, especially if the garment is left in the laundry hamper for several days. Unfortunately, a cold-water wash will not efficiently remove the oils from the skin that land on dirty laundry. There is a scientific formula that can be applied to laundry; for more information, and a pie chart, go to www.laundrywisdom.com. Basically it is a chart, with a circle (pie), divided into four equal parts which are Time, Mechanical, Temperature, and Chemical. All four elements equal pie, if any one of the elements is reduced in intensity, on or more of the others must be increased. Example: Cold water wash(Temperature), then it needs to intensify on chemicals (laundry detergent) and a longer drying effect (mechanical) at higher heats at longer periods (Time).

4. Hang it out to dry. There are around eighty-eight million dryers in the United States; each one emits more than a ton of carbon dioxide per year. Because dryers use so much energy, not using a dryer at all makes a real and immediate difference. Clothes last twice as long when you hang dry because there is less wear and tear than when you use the dryer. If your only reason not to hang dry is because you don't like stiff clothes, please try the following: Add half a cup of salt or a quarter cup of baking soda to your washer, and use only two tablespoons of your favorite detergent. Instead of fabric softener, add half a cup of white vinegar. Please give this recipe a try. Another tip is to hang out heavy blankets and quilts out of a second-story window to air.

Maybe you don't line dry because you don't have the space, or your home owners association does not allow it, or your neighbors will complain (lucky you). If you cannot convert wholly to the clothesline method, for whatever reason, create a hybrid drying routine in which you still use your dryer but only half as much. Take clothes out of the washer and put them immediately on hangers and onto your shower rod. Hang wet clothes in closets, keeping them two to three inches apart. Hang clothes over doorways; hang them anywhere for part of the time and then finish the drying in the dryer. You will see a savings in your next electric or gas bill. If you think that this might be a little too much work, my friend Ruth has a retractable line. When it is rolled up, it is the size of a dinner plate; she hangs it on a hook and then pulls it through her dining room and living room and down the hall. Using one retractable clothesline and two small hooks, she dries a whole load of wash. It is awesome. It also acts as a humidifier in the winter months and air freshens her home. Instead of using those canned sprays or candles, hang the laundry up in your house, and it will smell of fresh, clean clothes. If you are going to stick with the dryer, clean the lint filter every time; this will increase its efficiency and shorten the drying time. Dry loads of laundry back to back, if possible, to keep your dryer from having to heat up again. Try, too, not to use dryer sheets; my own research has revealed that it takes up to two-thirds as long to dry a load with a fabric softener sheet than without one.

5. Don't iron if you don't have to. I really, really hate to iron. Not only is ironing a tedious job, it also consumes a lot of energy. Because no self-respecting environmentalist wants to look unpolished, there are alternatives to this extremely uncivil activity. To avoid ironing, follow these easy steps: hang up or fold clothes as soon as you take them from dryer or clothesline, and store them right away. My mom use to say, "Watch me. I am ironing with my hands. Your Nana Hahn taught me this." She would take her hands and fan them over the fabric she was folding, or when she was making a bed, she would iron the sheets with her hands. I fold shirts where I want the creases to be, and then place them neatly under other clothes in my bureau; the weight from the other clothes actually helps to press them. I am very careful when I buy new clothes so that I do not have to iron them. I have a few older items

that still need to be ironed after every wear. You put those nifty linen outfits on for fifteen seconds, and they look like you slept in them all night. Ah, but if I keep gaining weight, they will not fit me—a perfect excuse for finishing those chips I have been eyeing.

6. Use green or biodegradable laundry detergents. Choose concentrated detergents, which generally offer more cleaning power ounce for ounce, so you use less. Smaller containers are easier to carry and store. They also make a smaller carbon footprint; by using them, we are helping to save the environment. The huge bottles that are not concentrated are mostly watered-down detergent. I used to buy them, thinking I was saving a lot of money. Just trying to lug them around wasn't worth it. When I tried to pour a small amount into the cap, it felt like I was picking up a fifty-pound bag of grain. You don't have to pay extra for performance.

You do pay, however, for the convenience of liquids or premeasured packets. Some people buy detergents with the fabric softener added; they save money because you do not have to buy both products. I had a terrible time with these products and was relieved when the May 2008 *Consumer Reports* confirmed that they do not work very well as separate cleaners or softeners. You also have to be wary of products that are too small, for example, the little soap packets that claim to be six times stronger than regular detergent. When I used them, the clothes would have a filmy or slimy feeling after the wash was done. My wash never looked dingier.

When I started this project, I searched for and bought every detergent that was on the market. I have spent over two years trying different methods with different detergents. God bless my friends who jumped in to help me. I gave them unmarked bags and instructions for testing the products, and they always faithfully followed through. Their remarks encouraged me to keep testing some detergents and to throw out others. The most valid lesson I learned was that we all had different types of water. This may not seem like such a big thing, but it is extremely important. People with water softeners really should use fewer products. This doesn't only apply to laundry products but to every household cleaning product. Those who use well water, which is usually hard water, need to use a little bit more. I am surprised that manufacturers do not label their products based on the different water types. Have you ever tried a product and thought that it worked miracles? Then when you tell a friend, she comes back to you and says that "it was okay"? Guess what? It is the water.

The only mistake I made was with my own family. One day, I had the bright idea to offer to do my children and grandchildren's laundry. I thought that I would get some really grungy wash from my grandchildren on which to test products. The deal was my children had to drop off the dirty clothes on certain days and pick it up when I called later that day. Unfortunately, I had totally forgotten how much wash infants could generate. My house looked like a landfill on a good day. There were loads of wash everywhere you looked. I did get a good understanding of laundry detergent. The conventional detergents can contain ingredients that are harmful to you. There is a list as long as my arm; it just is too depressing to list them.

Whatever detergent you decide to use for your family, the biggest secret is to use less! I finally broke down and put a dollar-store tablespoon ring in my laundry room. I use one to two tablespoons of detergent per load. Every single time, my wash has come out cleaner. This is extremely important if you own a high-efficiency (HE) washer, which will not rinse clothes as well as an agitator model. The HE washer uses six gallons or less water to rinse, while the agitator model uses up to twenty-four.

Laundry Stain Removers

These products frequently contain alkylphenol ethoxylates (APEs), which are common surfactants. Surfactants, or surface active agents, are chemicals that make it easier to mix substances with water; they allow cleansers to penetrate stains quickly and wash them away. Stain removers also often have phosphates, which are used to enhance cleaning but can spur the growth of algae that negatively affect ecosystems very quickly. To ensure you are purchasing a nontoxic product, make sure the stain remover does not contain petroleum products, phosphates, chlorine, or synthetic fragrances and dyes; you can find a huge variety of brands at most supermarkets.

The one rule you have to stick to is to read the labels. When I started doing this, I quickly became annoyed. I neither knew what more than two-thirds of the ingredients were, nor could I even pronounce them. By the time I finished reading one label, I could have had two loads of wash done. I am convinced that there is a strategy behind the naming of these chemicals; some of the names are outrageous. I believe companies do it on purpose, so people will give up trying to figure out what they are and, worse yet, what they do. Ask someone what sodium dodecylbenzene sulphonate means. (It is found in heavy-duty detergents, and yes, it is bad.) As soon as the media makes a story out of one of these chemicals, the companies change the name.

For example, monosodium glutamate (MSG), a food enhancer, used to be found in much of Chinese food. Then it began showing up in everything, and people started to have violent reactions to it. We had a friend who was very allergic to MSG. We would go out to dinner, and Robert always asked if there was MSG in any of the food. One time at a fine food establishment, we had to rush him to the hospital. I told the doctor that the staff had told us there was no MSG. The doctor replied, "There wasn't any 'MSG.' Just last week I was reading in my medical journal, and they have eleven new names for MSG." When the FDA started to give manufacturers heat for using MSG and the public became aware and stopped buying products with that ingredient, companies came up with eleven new names—which, it turns out, is absolutely legal. There has to be a corporate hell somewhere.

Allergies

Incidences of asthma and allergic reactions are much higher than they were ten years ago. The number of infants with asthma has increased tenfold in the last twenty years. In 2005, the Centers for Disease Control reported that 6.5 million American children were affected by asthma. While genetics may hold some of the responsibility for those numbers, environmental exposure also seems to be a major cause. One theory, for example, is that fabric softeners are having a negative effect on infants. Not only do they contain artificial fragrances, but the most harmful chemicals are found in both the unscented and the scented versions. Fabric softeners and fabric sheets contain ethanol, which is on the EPA's hazardous waste list; ethyl acetate, a narcotic on the list; and chloroform, a neurotoxin, anesthetic, and carcinogen. Liquid fabric softener contains formaldehyde to keep that smell going all day. In addition, most dryer sheets are petroleum based. The list and the studies go on and on. What to do?

Like my dad always said, "Pay attention!" Follow instructions, and read the labels. Ingredients are listed in descending order with the most prominent listed first. For example, if water is first on the list, the product has more water in it than anything else. The last ingredient listed is present in the least amount. It is the same with food labels, which often give me a good chuckle. If something like basil dressing looks really good, but the last ingredient is basil, I know it isn't going to taste that good.

Never, ever overcompensate when using detergent or any laundry product. I have watched friends just dump the detergent in the washing machine. If they added that much conditioner to their hair, what would happen? They would have grease slicks on top of their heads. The same is true of your clothes. When you just pour in the fabric softener, or use three dryer sheets instead of one, you essentially are making the clothes filthier. If the label says "add a capful," then do that. I always use less than what the label says. If saving money is your major goal, make your own detergent. At the end of this book is a chapter of recipes with which I have found great success. Not only is this an economic savings, but it is fun, and I was surprised to see my whole family become involved with the process. Another suggestion is to replace fabric softener with baking soda. Just one half to three quarters of a cup tossed into the wash leaves clothes soft and smelling fresh. I also frequently add white vinegar to the washer. Distilled white vinegar contains 5 percent acetic acid and has a pH balance of about 2.4. Most laundry soaps have a pH that ranges between 8 and 10. The vinegar helps neutralize the pH; thus, it helps wash the soap out of fabrics, leaving clothes fluffier and softer than fabric softener does. Two of my three children unfortunately have psoriasis. Vinegar has worked miracles as a fabric softener for our family. Try it!

Now, you are probably wondering which detergent won our contest. My friends and I tested and retested more than sixty-seven laundry products for over two years. We looked at each product to determine the best in performance, price, and environmental safety. It turned out that I picked products based on their smell. I did not realize I was doing it at first. My friends pointed it out to me on several occasions. I absolutely love the lavender scent, which has been associated with laundry as far back as the Romans. Many of the lavender detergents I bought were in powder form. They were all very expensive. Most would be fine for delicates or hand washing, but not for everyday laundry. Most of my friends have desk jobs—in other words, they do not have to get dirty—and they settled for Method. The product that rated the highest was Green Works, made by Clorox. I wasn't even going to try it. When I first saw it, I really hesitated. The name Clorox does not make me think "natural." My attitude was, "Please, they have a green item. What a joke." In the end, the joke was on me. I never considered that Clorox would have the engineers and chemists who could do the job right. I have to say they did their homework. It is the company's first new laundry product on the market in twenty years. It works highest with my high-efficiency washer, mixes well with cold water, has no side effects, and does a safe job on baby clothes. I have to say, "Wow!" which in this case stands for "without work." Clorox also makes a spot remover that I am pleased with; it works extraordinarily well with toddler and husband set-in food stains. My sons once left their socks and moldy towels in the trunk of their car in ninety-degree heat for over three days. (I swear, I raised them better than that!) I decided to use Green Works, cold water, and one cup of white vinegar, and they came out perfect with the first wash. I have used this product for more than six months, and while I do get the moldy smell in the washer occasionally, it is not present nearly as much as it was before. The best part of the story is that I found the product that works best for my family.

CHAPTER FOUR

ALL ABOUT HIGH-EFFICIENCY WASHERS AND DRYERS

There are several types of high-efficiency (HE) washers and dryers on the market today. All of a sudden, HE washers and Energy Star logos are everywhere. In January 2007, the U.S. Department of Energy established requirements that washers use 21-percent less energy, a goal most people wholeheartedly supported.

Types of HE Washers

There are two types of HE washers, front load and top load. They have one thing in common: they use less water than traditional agitator washers. In front-load HE washers, the laundry tumbles back and forth through the water as the tub rotates clockwise and then counterclockwise, moving the water and soap. This repetitive motion does an efficient cleaning and rinsing job and is gentle on all fabrics. Top-load washers operate using a gentle motion, spinning, rotating, and wobbling wheels, plates, or disks to agitate the wash. Like front-load machines, some new top-loaders also spray or lightly shower clothes using re-circulated wash water. Top-loaders that are labeled HE use low-water volume wash cycles. They either have no center post or a smaller-sized center post instead of a traditional agitator. A front-loader is more water efficient than a top-load machine. A top-loader requires enough water to cover all of the clothes in its drum; a front-loader needs only a third of that amount because its drum is set horizontally in the machine. As the drum turns, gravity drops the clothes back down into the water. And while a top-load machine will empty the soapy water and refill for a rinse-agitation cycle, a front-loader just sprays clean water on the laundry as the drum continues to turn, saving gallons of water. Since there is no agitator in a front-loader, there is a lot more room for dirty clothes, and larger loads means fewer loads. The front-load machine's spin mechanism can reach up to 1,000 rpm as opposed to the standard top-loader's average of 650 rpm. That means less water remains in the finished laundry, which gives it a shorter drying time.

Space

If your laundry room is short on space, take accurate measurements before you go shopping. Measure the width and height in your laundry room. One option offered by a front-load machine is that you can stack the dryer on top of the washer. If floor space is important to you, a front-loader is the best choice.

Color of the machine

There are a limited number of color choices for HE washers and dryers: cherry red, bold blue, and stainless steel. Remember, too, that these colors probably will be out of style in a few years and thus will date your machine. I have heard that when one appliance needs to be replaced, the original color may no longer be available, and you will have to settle for a mismatch.

The darker the color, the easier it is to notice scratches, dents, and fingerprints. The colored washer and dryer that I looked each at cost $400 extra. I got the white; the color white not only is more economical, but it also is ageless and matches with everything. In addition, the stainless steel is not really stainless steel. Before making a purchase, find out the percentage of stainless steel in the product. I have heard numerous complaints about how hard it is to keep them clean. My first reply was to use stainless-steel cleaner, but that does not work very well. One woman told me that it takes more time to clean the front of her machines than it does to do her laundry.

Clothing has survived being beaten by agitators for more than fifty years, but there might be a better way. The front-loader is rated best when it comes to the care of clothes. Because it relies on gravity, it greatly reduces the wear and tear on the laundry. (Admittedly, I usually grow out of my favorite garments before they have a chance to be worn out by a washer.) Cost is a huge factor to take into consideration, and I would like to point out a few mistakes that I made in this department.

The front-load machines are significantly more expensive than the top-loaders, several hundred dollars more expensive. The sales person kept repeating that I would save in energy costs over the long run. That was mistake number one: I should have done the math. The truth is that I would have to live to the age of one hundred to see a difference. If your budget is $500 or less, get a top-loader. I purchased my machine with a one-year, no-interest loan. Mistake number two: I did not bother to ask how much the interest rate would increase after one year. Would you believe that it was 28 percent? If you do the math, it will surprise you. Another point that is important to consider: if you have any handicaps or have a problem bending or kneeling, stay with a top-loader. With a front-loader, you will need to bend and kneel while loading and removing the clothes. I also have a habit of adding to a load once it gets started. I always forget the kitchen towels, or the kids throw me a T-shirt. Once a front-loader starts, however, it is in lock-down, and you have to wait until the wash is done. My LG front-loader has a option that only allows me to add clothes during the first five minutes of a wash cycle. If you are buying a front-loader, make sure it has this option.

The Energy Star logo is recognized by most people. It represents a government-backed program that helps businesses and individuals "protect the environment through energy-efficient products and practices" (www.energystar.gov). For the greatest energy efficiency, buy an Energy Star–rated washer. Do not hesitate to compare energy guide figures; it can save you money in the long run. My LG is not an Energy Star appliance, but when manufacturer reps are speaking to you about energy efficiency, they are not talking about saving electricity or gas or water. Mistake number three, I believe, was the worst one. In my old machine, a normal load took twenty-eight minutes. Then, three years ago, I purchased my LG front-loader. My first load of laundry was a full normal load. It took fifty-five minutes to wash with no extra functions. For my next load, again, a normal-sized one, I decided to add an extra rinse, which took one hour and seven minutes. The same was true of my HE dryer. To this day, I cannot figure out why my LG appliances take twice as long as my old washer and dryer. I have contacted several experts, all of whom assure me that I am saving energy. My electric bill, however, has increased, not decreased. One company explained that I am saving electric power because it is an "overturn electric power, not under-turn power." When I asked a certified electrician about this, he dropped the phone, he was laughing so hard. He told me that there is no such thing. I went back to the company and asked to receive the theory via e-mail, so I could have it in writing. I am still waiting for a reply.

The manufacturers of these machines promise energy savings because their washers offer cold-water rinses rather than hot-water rinses. That does save energy, but I could have set my old washer to use cold water for every load. The manufacturers claim their washers save water, which they do. They are advertised as using as little as six to seventeen gallons of water while my old washer might have used forty-two gallons per load. The problem is that the companies forget to tell you that it is six gallons per *rinse*, not per load.

These are important questions that you need to ask before you buy. It may be that the front-load washers use more water, not less. In our area, for example, you no longer can buy a standard toilet; the only ones sold are "low flush," i.e., toilets that use less water per flush. Often, however, it takes more than one flush to clear the toilet. My husband shook his head in utter disbelief when the low-flush toilets hit the market. They actually use twice as much water as the old standard toilets because people have to flush them two or three times.

Mold in HE Washers

A moldy smell is a problem associated with front-load washing machines. The manufacturers are facing several class-action lawsuits. Every manufacturer that I talked to said the same thing: people use too much detergent. It also is important to use HE detergent. After all, would you use your liquid dish soap in the dishwasher? (In addition, if you use non-HE detergent, it could void your warranty.)

What causes the mold in your washer is the low water level, which results in wash residue; dirt, grime, and even skin flakes, along with water softeners, fabric softeners, and left-over detergent do not always fully drain from a front-loader. Using cold water for most loads can increase this problem threefold. Residue also can build up in the door's rubber gasket, soap and fabric-softener dispensers, or other major parts of your washer. Over a short period of time, mold can begin to form, or the washer will begin to smell.

Three months after I started using my front-loader, I noticed a moldy odor. With a little research, I found a lot of remedies for this problem. Here are some tips for preventing mold and odors in your washing machine. Please note, however, that what works for some machines, may not work for others.

1. Always leave the washer door and the dispenser unit slightly ajar after the laundry is done. It is essential that these parts dry out.
2. If you have to use a fabric softener, please use dryer sheets rather than liquid softener in the washer. Putting white vinegar in the fabric-softener dispenser has worked wonders for me and several of my readers.
3. After every load is done, always rotate the drum with your hand, and check for items that may have stuck to the top or sides. It is pretty dark inside the washer and sometimes hard to see if you have removed every piece of clothing.
4. HE icon detergents are formulated to have lower suds, easier to rinse out with less water. I had a tough time deciding the difference between regular detergent and HE approved. The only thing I could find is that the HE icon detergent is several dollars more. The HE icon on every detergent bottle is not trademarked or registered, and comes at no cost to the manufacture. It is up to each manufacture to formulate a safe biodegradable, low sudsing environmentally friendly product. I can name several products that are not doing this. What gets my goat is that the warranty to my HE washer insists that I use an HE-approved product. The joke is that there is nobody that officially approves any HE product on the market today!
5. Use less detergent than recommended. I cannot emphasize this enough. Experiment until you find a minimum measurement that gives you a clean wash. Start with one tablespoon and work up from there. The tumble action of high-efficiency washers creates more suds, which are harder to rinse out, than do the agitator action of old traditional washers.

6. You occasionally will have to use hot water, particularly with whites or towels. If you have babies, always use hot water. The hot water also will clean the residue build-up in the washer. (See also the section on washing in cold water in chapter 3.)

7. Check the gasket inside the door for loose dirt and hair. I always wipe it dry with a cotton tea towel to speed up the drying process. My LG has a door at the bottom that you can remove and clean out. This is an excellent feature.

8. Read the manual to see the manufacturer's suggestions for cleaning the washer. HE front-loaders have a cleaning or maintenance cycle—during which you'll complete a full wash cycle without any clothes in the machine—and it is imperative that you use it periodically. Manufacturers recommend that you perform this maintenance as often as once a week or, at minimum, once a month. Check the use-and-care guide for your model. If you have a question, please call the manufacturer's toll-free, customer-service number. Sometimes you have to wait, but it is worth it to get the right information for your machine.

I have gotten a ton of e-mails with suggestions for removing the moldy smell, from Clorox to vinegar. They all work for a couple of wash loads; then the smell is back. If you have a moldy smell in your front-loader, I cannot express the importance of resolving the matter as quickly as possible. If you let it go, it could lead to severe health problems.

Here are some tips that I have worked for me. For some reason, known only to the brightest chemist, some of these formulas will work on some machines and not on others. (Contact your manufacturer if you cannot get rid the moldy odors; some warranties will enable you to replace your machine.) These are directions for the periodic shock treatments suggested by washing machine manufacturers.

Chlorine treatment

Add one to two cups of liquid bleach directly to the empty tub. Run the longest, hottest cycle available on your machine. According to scientists, chlorine acts by burning the cell walls of the mold or mildew; then, the cells rupture and they die. This method only affects the very top surface of the mold or mildew build-up. It must be repeated as needed. It requires running an extra-large, hot-water cycle with no clothes in the tub.

While this method can be effective in killing mold organisms, it also attacks the seals and gaskets of the machine. The amount of chlorine needed to control mold growth can be much more than the amount needed to brighten laundry. Thus, the machines are not designed to handle too much of this type of shock. This is similar to the chlorine shock that is used in swimming pools; the water becomes clear, but the walls are slippery.

Small black flecks and or small globs of goo in the clothes are an indication that the seal has failed and that some of the waterproof grease has leaked into the drum.

Baking Soda and Vinegar Treatment

Please read this carefully! Never add vinegar and baking soda to the machine at the same time, or you will get a super mess. First, add one or two cups of baking soda directly to the empty tub. Add the vinegar during the final rinse or into the softener dispenser. Run the longest, hottest cycle available on your machine. Baking soda increases the ph balance, and vinegar decreases it. This may affect the growth of the mold and mildew build-up; however, I have been told by several readers that the baking soda does not work. One gentleman told me to use one or two quarts of white vinegar only and the hottest possible cycle. I used two quarts of white vinegar, and it has worked wonders. The recipe that the LG reps gave to me is as follows. They suggested that I do this once a week, even when I think I have no odors. Use two cups of white vinegar and two cups of bleach. Do not mix these together, ever! Fill the soap dispenser with the vinegar. Let the washer fill up with the hottest temperature water. Let it soak for one to six hours; I let it sit overnight. Then restart the washer, and let it run a complete cycle. Immediately repeat the same process, this time without any vinegar. Instead, use two cups of bleach. It took me two days to do this procedure, and I could not believe they were telling me to do it once a week. But it worked. The customer-service rep told me that this is what I would have to do in exchange for using cold-water to wash most of my laundry. I asked, "So you are telling me that if I used hot water for all of my laundry, I would not have to service my machine like this?" The answer was, "Yes, but you would no longer be energy efficient!"

Commercial Cleaners

The commercial products on the market now cost more than $8 each. I tried them and did not get the results I expected. When I called the company for advice, I was told to use the product several times to get results. At $8 a pop plus the expense of heating the water, what was I saving, again? Oh, yes, that's right—water! I have used a 1.5-liter bottle of Listerine. It has worked wonders for me, although I do smell the mouthwash in several loads of wash after I use it. Please use at your own risk. Call your manufacturer to make sure it will not harm your washer. Listerine has a high alcohol content and may cause damage. Since it is safe to use as a mouthwash and it does kill bacteria, I felt comfortable putting it in my machine.

CHAPTER FIVE

EXERCISE THE BODY AND MIND

[T]he two kinds of people on earth, I mean,
Are the people who lift, and the people who lean.
—Ella Wheeler Wilcox

Always do right. This will gratify some people and astonish the rest.
—Mark Twain

No matter how you do it, laundry gives you a workout. And those who use a Laundromat really get a workout. In addition to burning calories, laundry can represent a spiritual journey as well. It allows people to have time to be alone and meditate, which many find so essential. Folding clothes, sorting and organizing, and moving heavy clothes from one area to the next; squatting, bending, and stretching when you hang your clothes. These activities engage the lower and upper body. Doing laundry can be a low-impact aerobic activity.

Bend and stretch from the waist while picking up laundry or objects from the floor. Really squat when you pick things up; don't bend over. Slowly pick up a basket with wet laundry, and lift it to your waist. Put it back down with your arms extended. Once again, slightly bend and lift it up to your waist. Work up to twenty-five repetitions. Stretch each time you hang an article of clothing on the line. Stand on your toes as long as you can. When sorting laundry, kick one leg back as far as you can and hold. Switch legs and repeat. I kicked my dog doing this, so make sure no one is around. When folding laundry, stand up and shift your body weight from side to side. This extra movement may seem silly, but it adds movement, which burns calories. A man by the name Alex Gadsden invented a bicycle-powered washer called the Cycleclean. It has no electric power and runs while he bikes. Now that is going green! I call my exercise Crank Up the Music, and I dance around the laundry room to really good tunes. Yes, I seriously do this. You have to be creative and make exercise a way of life.

I had heard that there is something called a no-sweat exercise. This sounded really intriguing to me, so I researched it. It turns out that no-sweat exercise is "stress"! (Isn't it funny that stress rhymes with mess?) Everyone I know uses the word frequently. I believe half of it is due to advertising: "Are you stressed about keeping your house clean? Try this miracle snake oil, and your stress will melt away." Remember that old commercial, "Calgon, take me away," where a woman in a bath tub looked so relaxed she seemed to be three steps from heaven. We all have problems and "those days." Even the rich and famous experience it, probably more than we do. I do think, however, that the word stress is overused. It is a side effect of technology; there is so much to learn just to keep up with daily life. (To be honest, I cannot even begin to work the video machine or the DVD player. My children can text their friends at the same time they are carrying on a conversation with me. I take so long to type the first letters, the phone turns off.)

I have so much on my mind that sometimes I get belligerent and say, "No more!" You practically have to go to school to learn how to use modern appliances. These days, instead of a 120-page manual, a product now comes with a DVD. After you finish watching it, you still can't find the product's on switch.

The second lesson that I have learned is the simple act of slowing down. They say that by slowing down and engaging in repetitive activities that require complete attention on the movement direct you to focus on your physical self. And the stress eases or disappears. In another words, just forget your problem or whatever is stressing you out and come back to it at another time. One woman hangs her wash just to stop trying to make up her mind. She claims that her biggest task in life is to decide how, where, and why she should do something. In short, she is always trying to make up her mind.

There are seemingly millions of self-help books on the market today, each of which claims to have the secret to a happier life. The so-called experts say that if you eat this, or exercise in that way, or stand on your head, you will be a happier and more balanced individual. There are rooms filled with scientists trying to figure out how the brain works.

I have concluded that it just boils down to relying on common sense and finding simple ways of dealing with situations. I have to remind myself to apply these lessons constantly. People I have interviewed have told me, overwhelmingly so, that they just want to be happy. It is no secret that it is our attitudes that make us feel happy. Every day that we wake up, we run into all kinds of situations. We can decide to think about the unhappy events that life hands to us, or we can relish the happy times. We become slaves to our thoughts, and often those thoughts are negative. We replay through our minds, What if I said? And how would they like it if I did? Three days later, you are stuck on the same problem, and in many instances, everyone around you is sick of hearing about it.

What is happiness? Remember my story about Jack in the first chapter? The outdoor smell of freshly dried clothes made him happy. When his world was closing him down, he relied on that memory to make him happy. Happiness is a feeling of inner peace, when we do something we really love or get what we want. For some people, happiness is seeing something they appreciate—the first snow flakes, the first spring foliage. Holidays bring joy to many people, for they are times spent celebrating with family and friends. For some people, happiness is fast and fleeting; for them, it usually comes only by purchasing materialistic items, like a new dining room set or a new couch. It is fine if this is an occasional purchase, but if you find yourself constantly buying big ticketed items or becoming a shopaholic, put on the brakes now!

One of the best ways to keep being happy is to find time for meditation on a daily basis. I like to refer to it as the "joy habit." It does not have to be long, and it can be achieved in so many different ways. Pick what works for you. Look at what you have done, not at what you have not been able to do. Some days I fall off the tracks; I just do not accomplish what I have set out to do. There is always tomorrow. Be realistic about what you are going to accomplish. After trying to play super mom for years, I thought I was over it, and then I became super grandmom. On some days, do a random act of kindness to make others happy. There is a great book called *Practice Random Acts of Kindness*, with a foreword by Rabbi Harold Kushner, which states that when you make someone happy, you are happy and, in return, people try to make you happy.

On some days, treat yourself, perhaps by eating something you like—forget the calories—going for a walk, or watching a great movie. Listen to music that you like. Pay attention to your thoughts. Whenever you feel yourself sliding back into negative thoughts, start thinking of pleasant ones.

Go outside and play; I am sure we all have heard that before. I can remember my mom screaming it, "Go out and play." One day at the doctor's office, I picked up the December 2008 issue of *Psychological Science*. I was astonished to discover that there are serious scientific studies on play. Feeling like you have brain drain, and you can't concentrate? Psychologists have now found out that interaction with nature, even in the cold, makes you a bit smarter. In other words, I now can say that if you hang your laundry outside, it actually will make you a smarter person. Yes, indeed! The article has only one big flaw; it states that communing with nature works but not while you are in the city. The studies showed that when you take a walk in a city, your mind still is locked on the workload. The same thing happened when they showed people pictures. Those of nature helped people relax, but pictures with skyscrapers did not. Pictures of nature will attract your "involuntary attention." Something captures your attention because it interests you. What is interesting varies from person to person. As one researcher noted, people don't generally claim that looking at waterfalls makes them tired. The researchers only tested nature-based and urban walks. They did not test visiting museums or hanging laundry. I have always loved the outdoors, and I am always amazed at what nature has to offer. No matter where we live, we all have one thing in common: nature surrounds us. I have to disagree with the scientists who state that city dwelling is not nature friendly. Nature does not stop at the city limits; you just have to look a little harder. Some of us see the shape of the clouds, while others will feel the warmth of the sun, and still others hear the birds.

One moment that I will cherish forever happened on what started out as an ordinary day. I was carrying out baskets of laundry with my chattering nineteenth-month-old granddaughter, Ava. We started to hang clothes. Her job was to pull the laundry out of the basket and hand it to me. Suddenly she said, "Mimi, look up, look up." I looked up and saw perfect clouds, the kind that artists try to capture. Ava immediately lay down next to the laundry basket and pointed her chubby finger to the sky. "See, Mimi, see?" I lay down next to her and stared at the sky. It was exquisite. I thought about how I rarely looked all the way up into the sky. I look down plenty. I look sideways, but I never look straight up. How much do you miss when you look straight ahead? The laundry was wet in the basket, but I did not care. I had so many things on my agenda that day, but I did not care. At least twenty minutes went by, as we lay on the ground, staring at the clouds. Ava jumped up to chase the cat, Wilma, who had quietly snuck up to see what we were doing. In her munchkin voice, Ava said, "Come here, Wilma, come here." I continued to lie lazily on the ground for a few more moments and breathe in the fresh air. Sometimes you just have to stop what you are doing, and step outside yourself. Being too busy is never a justifiable excuse. Nature is always there to take you by the hand.

Praying is another great way to spiritually heal oneself. It does not matter what religion you believe in or what God you pray to. Prayer is a powerful tool. There is no place better than the clothesline to reflect in prayer. Spiritual growth is an important inner process; it promotes a happier, fuller life, free of fear and anxiety.

Sometimes you have to dismiss friends and family members who offer nothing but constantly negative thoughts. I imagine this is a step people go through when they get divorced or when a loved one dies. People I love very much become vampires of my energy. It takes courage to say no more, and move on. As you move through a new spiritual world, you will learn to rise above frustration, disappointment, and negative feelings. You will become more tolerant and patient. You will become better caretakers of the world. My number-one rule is to open the door to the positive and close the door on negative. Be grateful for what you do have and not for what you want.

CHAPTER SIX

TEACH YOUR CHILDREN FROM TODDLER TO TEEN

Children are our national treasure. With what measure we give to them in their childhood, they will give to our nation in their lifetime.
—Pearl S. Buck

I certainly could not have phrased it any better. Children become adults all too quickly. In the blink of an eye, they are grown. When my children were younger, we would be standing in line at the grocery store, and a senior citizen would say to me, "Oh, they grow so quickly. Enjoy it while you can." I would smile back and thank them, but I thought to myself, "Are you kidding me? Just today, this one sprayed my kitchen down with pesticide to rid himself of his little sister, and this little darling one here has kept my husband and I awake for seven full years." I wasn't aware of it, but I was so stuck in the moment, I could not find one thing pleasurable about my children. Today, thirty years later, I am the woman in the line, telling young mothers, "Oh, they grow so fast. Enjoy it while you can."

Children who learn to respect the natural world tend to be kinder and more accepting of their fellow human beings. Hopefully, they also learn to be less materialistic, more resourceful, more concerned with a social and environmental justice, less selfish, and better able to think on their own and on a larger scale.

Teaching Green

Teaching children to go green definitely will make a colossal difference in just one generation. Teaching your children how to cook something besides cookies and other sweets will benefit their future. My kids taught me more about recycling than I could have imagined, even though I was brought up on recycling. Those were the good old days, when you returned your soda bottles and burned your trash in the fifty-five-gallon drum behind the garage. When I left home, I left my recycling habits behind and started to throw everything into the garbage. I did not even realize I was doing this until my children were learning about recycling in school. I can still remember hearing the story about the poor ducks that got their heads stuck in one of those plastic-ring six-pack holders. My daughter made me cut them into a hundred pieces.

One habit that I did not leave at home was laundry. It is never too early to teach your children to help with the laundry. Children today think that the only use for a clothespin is to snap it on to a snack bag! Whether they are boys or girls, they need to learn how to do laundry. I have friends that strongly disagree with me. They believe they were overworked by their own parents when they were children: "I am not going to do to my children what my mom did to me." They completely miss my point. I am not sending Junior down to the riverside to do the family wash. But if you don't show them how everyday chores are done, they will not learn life's valuable lessons. At some point in your children's development, you will meet that scary parent who explains that her child is so highly intelligent, she will not waste time teaching him chores. When her child gets older, he will have people to pick up after him. "Okay" is all I can say when I meet people like this. You have to give these parents one point for "positive thinking," but also subtract thirty points because they are too lazy to teach their own children.

I began by teaching my own children to sort laundry when they were toddlers. They all enjoyed this job until they were maybe five years old. Then, it would start. "Not now, Mom." Sometimes, it seemed easier to do it myself. But, parents, you cannot do everything for your children. I realized that I'd expected them to do it exactly as I had done it. It was a big step for me to learn that, no, they could not fold clothes just like me, not at first; I had to practice patience. I couldn't yell at them if their work did not rise to my level of excellence. As long as they gave it their best shot, I had to be proud of that.

Establish rules, and stick to them. If they ever are going to be responsible adults, kids need to learn how to do laundry—not every once in a while but as an everyday chore. Picking up their clothes every day is the first rule. Explain, not just once but all the time, why they need to pick up their own clothes and toys. Have them assist you with each step. They will slowly pick up and develop a habit of it (you hope).

For years, I hung on my refrigerator the following saying: "Kid power is the largest untapped source of energy in the world." Children have the ability at a very young age to come up with the best excuses, explanations for why they can't just do that chore at this moment. I thought I had heard them all at one time or another. "But Mom, that's not fair!" "I can't, it's too heavy!" Kids will give you excuses till the day they move out. My father had a few good comebacks that I am sure others have heard. One was, "Money does not grow on trees!" When we got older, he moved on to, "Time is like money. You don't find it, you make it." And finally, "Give thanks for the clothes on your back."

Here are a few tips for teaching your children how to do laundry. If your children are between the ages of eight and twelve, please do not try to teach them everything at once. Add a new skill each time you do the laundry together. If the child is a quick learner, and demands to do it all on his or her own, step back and watch closely for a couple of weeks. I insist on sticking to green or natural products, even if they want to use bleach. Furthermore, I never allow them to be unsupervised. When my kids were teenagers and had friends visiting, there were moments when they acted sillier than a two-year-old. A doctor once told me, "That kind of thinking is caused by hormones." Expect accidents to occur every once in a while. They happen to me, even after all the laundry I have done: A wool sweater ends up in the dryer. I use too much bleach and ruin a couple of items. The list goes on. Expect kids of any age to have accidents.

I do think it is unfair to make your child do *all* the laundry. If a child does do the family laundry, however, he or she should receive a weekly allowance. Kids can be very creative, and they do come up with great ideas. Let them try out some of their ideas on their own. Last but not least, praise them for a job well done.

Laundry Steps

Don't worry that children never listen to you; worry that they are always watching you.
—Robert Fulghum

Step 1. Develop a laundry day or time that fits best with everyone's schedule. Set up basic rules for laundry. I started by keeping recipe cards or three-by-five-inch cards, stored in an old recipe box, with the laundry items. An example of a rule is: ask permission to run small loads for laundry. Try to discourage the children from doing small loads. For example, if your son has a favorite pair of pants and insists that he must wear it to school every day, I would not allow him to wash it every day. How dirty are the pants? Check to see if they can be hung up and whether they really need laundering. Are there clothes belonging to other family members that the child can add to his load? It is important to set guidelines.

Towels can be one load; whites another load; brights and colors the last one. Make your own rules about which products you feel comfortable using, from the type of stain remover to the brand of detergent. Create a child-friendly laundry area. Ensure that the older children can get to the products without making it unsafe for the younger ones.

Step 2. A child of any age can help you with the laundry. I let them pull things out of the basket for me to fold before they can walk. I used to set the machines and let my children aged five or younger push the button or pull the knob to get them started. Write down the temperatures and cycles that you use for all different types of laundry. Make one list for the washer and one for the dryer. If your children are old enough to read, you will teach them how to use the machines rather quickly.

Step 3. Teach them how to sort as they get older, but go through this stage rather slowly. This is the number-one area for problems to arise and accidents to begin. As you sort the clothes, explain the different piles for whites, delicates, wools, leather, and other hard-to-wash or nonwash fabrics. Make it a rule to check the pockets for forgotten items. Toddlers love zipping up pants, but teens need to be reminded to zip up their jeans and pants before putting them in the washer. Tell them to check for stains. Make sure that they've turned all clothes right-side out before they put them in the washing machine. When hanging clothes outside on the line, a lot of people like to turn their colors to the wrong side, so they will not fade in the sun. Read the care labels with the children. It is a great way to teach the child the facts about a garment.

Step 4. Teach them to hand wash items that need it, such as delicates. Introduce them to stain remover. Decide which product is best for your family. Soak something overnight so the children can see how it is done. My children thanked me for showing them this task. When they got older and traveled, they found it very handy.

Step 5. Introduce the washing machine, which can be confusing, even to children who "know everything." Go through the steps and, again, put them on a recipe card. On the card, include the following: how much laundry makes a full load; how much is too small of a load; how to load the laundry, especially towels, so the washer remains balanced. Show them your choice of detergents, and where you put the detergent and fabric softener or vinegar. Show them how to use a stain stick or spray wash, and tell them not to use the whole stick or bottle on one item. Show them when to use hot, cold, or warm water. If you decide to let them use bleach, set some guidelines, e.g., use the recommended amounts, operate the machines in a safe manner, etc.

Step 6. Teach them how to use the dryer. Show the children where the lint trap is and how to clean it before each us. Remind them that when the dryer is finished, that some items like zippers and buttons can be very hot to the touch.

Teach the children how to shake the laundry as they take it from washer to dryer or line. Teach them to examine the damp laundry, and look for clothes that should never go into the dryer. Hanging clothes is easy because everything can go on the line.

Teach them the skill of hanging. My husband put in a children's line that was halfway down the pole so the young ones could reach and hang their own laundry by the time they were three years old. I still have the line today and use it with my grandchildren. My grandson, Mordecai, is fourteen months old and great at hanging socks. If you do not have an outdoor line, teach the children how to hang clothes on a folding rack. Show them how to reshape and form sweaters so they dry nicely.

Step 7. Teach them how to fold and put away their clothes immediately in their closets and drawers. One huge mistake I made with my kids was that I did not follow this step through to the end. They loved doing the laundry, but putting the clothes away was a nightmare. They would take the basket, put it in the bedroom, and then leave it there. Worse yet, they would throw wet towels or dirty laundry into the clean basket. They would just pull out the item they wanted to wear, and destroy the rest. They would have dressed using clothes from the laundry basket all week, if I'd let them. Several times, I walked into their rooms and felt like I needed to seek medical attention. Take it from me, make them put it all away when they take the baskets to their rooms.

Going Off to College: Laundry Instructions

All children are gifted; it is that just some open their packages earlier then others.
—Author unknown

When our first child went off to college, I tried not to have an anxiety attack, worrying about whether he would survive. Never did it cross my mind, however, that he might have a problem with laundry. I thought I had covered all bases: to use the ATM card for other things besides pizza, the importance of homework. I had visions of him out partying with his friends all night and blowing off all responsibilities. But the first phone call we got was when he wanted to know "how do you turn the washing machine on?" And, of course, "I need more money." I guess the $37-a-month allowance I'd budgeted didn't work out. When all three of my children hit "teenhood," it was like someone else had taken over their brains. I can remember having to chase them down to do household tasks. My son, especially, would balk, but I always told him, "I am not coming with you when you leave. Now get in here, and put this laundry away." He would smirk and say, "I am never going to leave." I should be grateful that his first call came after one week rather than three months!

I have designed a laundry list for freshman college students. Keep in mind, every college campus is different. I realized this when my other two children went off to college. Now, colleges give students a card similar to a credit card, which they use to buy meals and books or do their laundry. The parents are billed at the end of the semester. I guarantee you will either need a martini or an oxygen tank before you look at the bill.

Things You'll Need
- laundry detergent
- detergent dryer sheets (optional)
- change quarters or ID card
- stain remover
- iPod (it helps encourage them to stay at the Laundromat)
- laundry hamper (pop-up type)
- a laundry basket or two (perhaps a collapsible container or a duffel bag)
- hangers
- drying rack

Simple Steps of Dorm Laundry
- Always bring your room key.
- Try to avoid multiple trips.
- Pack a small bottle of detergent, which is easier to carry. Pick the type of detergent that does all types of laundry and whose smell you like.
- Never use dish soap, shampoo, or anything else in place of detergent; it will not work.
- A stain-remover stick works well. Keep one in your basket at all times. When you get a stain, apply the stick as soon as you can. Or use shaving cream; this will work, too, and is inexpensive. Use a bleach pen on whites only and wash the clothes immediately afterward.
- Empty all pockets, and unravel your balled-up clothes. A pen, tissue, or lipstick can absolutely ruin your day if it goes through the wash. If you throw your clothes into the washer in balls (sleeves inside out, one jean leg out the other in a knot and so on), your clothes will not

wash or dry correctly. Unfolded clothes also make refolding clean clothes much easier.

- Lugging your laundry. Some colleges permit students to keep a wagon. Ask the administration if this is allowed. A wagon with sides makes it a lot easier to move laundry, unless, of course, you are stuck with stairs. One of my children's favorite laundry devices for moving their wash, was a cart that was specially made for moving laundry baskets. I got it off the internet at breezedryers.com. It also came in very handy for moving other items back and forth from the dorm room. It folds for easy storage and fits under the dorm bed or in closet. Many kids use black trash bags to haul their laundry. This is not a good idea as the bags rip and tear and are a lot more expensive than a laundry basket. They are great for covering your wash if you have to go outside. If so, keep two trash bags on the bottom of the baskets in case it rains or snows.
- If you misplace or lose your laundry basket, use a belt. Roll your dirty laundry into a bundle, and strap the belt in the center. Carry the bundle using the end of the belt. Make sure that small and personable things are tucked safely in the center. The last thing you want to do is to leave a dirty trail of laundry.
- Try to get washers that are right next to each other. Do your laundry at off times, e.g., in the middle of the day when everyone else is in class. I do not recommend, however, doing laundry at 2 AM. Your brain needs to sleep!
- Leave a basket, or something else that is big enough to see from a distance, on top of every washer you use. This way, if you have to use washers at separate ends of the room, you will be able to locate your machines easily. There is nothing worse than arriving in your dorm room and noticing that you're missing your favorite jeans.
- Never leave your laundry unattended. I say this from experience. Every single college suffers from stealing. Some thieves steal not out of necessity but for fun. You may be lucky and be able to create a safe situation. For example, my daughter and her friends arranged a schedule; three or four of them would do their wash at the same time. They took turns staying with the wash and ended up all folding at the same time. Choose whatever system works for you, but please never leave your wash unattended.

- Separate your clothes; separate the whites from the darks and fine washables. Whites generally are washed in hot water; on some washers, you can choose a cold-water rinse, which saves energy. Darks are not to be washed in hot water, unless you've been working with funky microbacteria in biology. Hot water will shrink an item, especially if it is made of cotton. Check the garment label if you are unsure. Garment labels are there for a reason; please read them. When you are separating clothing, sometimes you will come across an item that is tough to sort: does it go with whites or colors? A striped shirt is one example. Always check the label, but generally I use the cooler wash temperature when I am not sure.
- Hand wash fine washables. I also suggest hand washing all new clothes. One of my favorite colors is bright green; I hand wash clothes in that color, too. You can do this in a sink.
- Remember to turn all of your clothes right-side out, and make sure that you've really checked all the pockets.
- Start the washer as directed. Do not start all of the machines at once; give yourself a few minutes in-between each load. You are not an octopus who can empty all the machines at once.
- Do not overload the machines. They definitely will not wash your clothes properly if you fill them with too many clothes.
- Add the detergent, but not too much. Remember, it is like using too much shampoo in your hair. Your hair will look greasy, and so will your clothes. Some people add fabric softener at this point. I would prefer you to use dryer towels instead.
- Then wait; you generally will have about thirty-five minutes to hang around. Please do not leave your laundry unattended. Hey, I have a great idea. Why don't you start your homework?
- When your clothes are completely washed, it is time to get your dryers in line. The same rules apply. Leave a laundry basket near each one that you use. Remove lint from the lint screen before you start. Note that some modern commercial dryers do not have lint screens.
- Add your clothes and a dryer sheet to the dryer.
- Take your fine washables and let them air dry on a rack. You may be able to put some clothes on hangers, and let them air dry.

Never overfill a dryer; it will take forever for the clothes to dry completely.

- Please check the garment label if you are unsure which dryer settings to use. Check and double-check the settings before you push the start button.
- Now, you'll have to wait again, usually between thirty minutes and an hour. Great! That means more time for homework.
- When the dryers are done, try to remove clothes immediately. The more time they have to sit and cool down, the more likely they are to wrinkle. Double-check the dryer for socks or other small items that you may have missed. Clean out the lint trap again for the next person.
- Fold the clothes immediately. Do not throw them into the basket with plans to fold later. Folding takes only a few minutes. Anyone who does not fold his or her clothes stands out like a sore thumb. Next time you are in a boring lecture, look around; you'll be able to tell who folds and who doesn't.
- If you have any further questions, give your mom or dad a call. Believe me, they will be glad to hear from you.

CHAPTER SEVEN

MAKE YOUR OWN
LAUNDRY PRODUCTS

I find the harder I work, the more luck I seem to have.
—Thomas Jefferson.

Do homemade laundry products really work? I have had countless conversations about this subject. Yes, they do, and no, they don't. Again, a major factor is your water. If you have hard water, it seems that the liquid formula will not work, but the powdered formula will. I have known women who use the exact same formula; one says it's fabulous, and the other says it leaves her whites dingy. They do have one thing in common: they save money. The laundry-products market in the United States is huge. Just detergent alone is a $130-billion business. No wonder the laundry aisle at the supermarket has such a gigantic selection. Often, however, the homemade product works better than the most expensive brands on the market. The expensive products are not always the best.

One woman told me that she is never going to go back to the manufactured brands because now she gets to call the shots. She explains that it is hard to make a choice in the supermarket because the manufacturers have mixed so many products together, such as detergent and fabric softener; added brighteners for dark clothing only; or created detergents just for whites. She states that the final straw was the addition of Febreze to detergents. Besides the fact that she does not like the smell of Febreze, she adds, "Are we not washing our clothes to gain freshness, not adding another scent?" Do you really save money making your own? The answer to this is definitely yes. You can save a lot of money, depending on the recipe that you choose. The time to create your own will be well spent.

Make Your Own Dryer Sheets

Let us start with the people who do not want to give up their fabric sheets. They have been educated about what is in them, and yet they still prefer to use them. This is fine; this is what freedom is all about. Here are a few ideas for those of you who like dryer sheets. A lot of people say to cut them in half; if you buy a box that holds eighty, it becomes a box of 160. This sounds great in theory, but it did not work for me. The little sheet curled up, and I had static cling. However, when I experimented with these products, I was not using vinegar or baking soda in my wash. Other people told me that the clothes just did not smell as fresh.

Another suggestion is to pour fabric softener into a spray bottle, and spray an old, clean rag three to four times. Then add it to the dryer with the wet clothes. One fabric-softener-soaked rag should last anywhere from four to six loads. After that, you must wash the rag, or it will start to smell funky. That's the beef fat beginning to turn on you. I tried this, and it did work, but I like this next idea much more. Take a damp washcloth, add ten drops of an essential oil of your preference (mine was lavender and mint).While the fragrance was great, it did not work against static cling. I tried adding five drops of vinegar to the dryer rag; that did not work either. But when I added the vinegar to the wash load, it worked.

Make Your Own Spot Remover

Fill a spray bottle with water to about three inches from the top. Then fill it to the top with your favorite laundry detergent. Screw on the lid, and shake gently. This idea got a C- from me because you have to shake the bottle each time you use it. It worked great for fresh stains that I could get to in a mini-second, but it did not work at all with set-in stains.

I prefer to use white vinegar, which works well with hard water and decreases the suds in detergent. I find it to be the best fabric softener; add one-half cup to a load of wash. White vinegar is also at the top as a disinfectant; it kills bacteria and works best on baby clothes. It works best on all types of odors, including those caused by mildew and socks. It is the best agent against perspiration stains. Finally, it can clean the washing machine; I set my machine for a large load, pour a whole gallon of vinegar into the washer, set it at hot water, and push the button. I have been using vinegar for more than four years in my HE washer and have never had a problem. The company that sold me my LG Tromm machine also recommends using vinegar in its HE machines. I have talked to reps at other companies that do not. My sister's HE is a Kenmore, and the salesman said not to ever use vinegar. She has had it for two years and has not had a problem. It is up to you to determine what makes best.

Hydrogen peroxide is another option. A 3-percent solution makes an awesome bleaching agent. I use it on my delicate antique tablecloths; it is also excellent for cleaning stains made by babies. A bottle of hydrogen peroxide will lose its effectiveness over time.

Club soda is the best stain remover for fresh stains; blot it lightly on the stain. I keep a small bottle with my laundry supplies. Club soda also will lose its effectiveness after about three to four months.

You can find a Fels-Naptha laundry bar in almost any supermarket store. If your store does not have it, ask the manager to get it. I have never paid more than $1.50 per bar in the store, although on the Internet, a bar sells for $6 and up. The best way to use the bar is to moisten the area of the garment where the stain has set. Run the Fels-Naptha bar under the faucet. It does not matter which temperature you choose. Rub the bar right onto the item, and work up a soapy lather. Then throw the item right into the washing machine, and wash it immediately. Fels-Naptha is one of Bubby's (my daughter-in-law's ninety-year-old grandmother) favorite stain removers. It also works great if you have a perspiration problem; follow the same instructions for set-in stains. Fels-Naptha is highly recommended by many people who make their own laundry products.

I keep a container of salt with my laundry products as well. Salt is great item to add to the wash if you use an outdoor clothesline in cold temperatures. I also use a half cup of salt in the washer every time I wash towels; it keeps them from getting stiff. Salt mixed with real lemon juice will get rid of mildew stains.

Lemon juice is known as nature's disinfectant and a natural bleach. I have always used real lemon juice. I recently purchased Minute Maid lemon juice, which is available in the frozen section of your supermarket.

I keep the thawed juice in my refrigerator. It works just as well as the real fresh lemon juice. Shelf-stable lemon juice products do not work for me. I have tried them on several occasions, and they did not even come close to the real lemon.

Baking soda is known to soften your wash; add a quarter of a cup of baking soda to the wash cycle, and your clothes will be as soft as snow. Our dermatologist told me to soak stinky socks in a solution of a quarter of a cup of baking soda and one gallon of water. Let them soak for two hours or more; do not rinse, wring out by hand, and dry. It sounds like a lot of work, but it really kills the odor. One whiff of those boys' socks, and believe me you will do this procedure every time you wash their socks. Baking soda is an excellent odor remover.

Borax is my favorite all-around laundry aid. It is gentle, cleans and deodorizes, and really helps get out set-in stains. It is also a water softener. Borax often is used with detergent as a boost for heavily soiled loads. I use a quarter of a cup of borax and two to three tablespoons of my liquid detergent in warm water and soak for thirty minutes. You can also apply the borax and detergent right to the washer. It is safe for HE machines.

This helpful hint comes from Bubby: shaving cream works better than any other spot and stain remover on the face of the earth. Shaving cream is whipped soap. Moisten the area that has the stain, and shoot a little shaving cream onto the spot. Work into a lather, and remove with a wet wash cloth. I use it for a carpet cleaner and a spot remover on furniture fabric. I always keep a can of shaving cream with my laundry products.

Homemade Recipes

Here are a few recipes that only need one or two ingredients.
- To make fabric softener and combat static cling, use half a cup of white vinegar in the wash cycle.
- To make fabric softener, add a quarter cup of vinegar to the wash cycle.
- To get rid of mold, use a quarter cup of borax plus enough water to cover the clothes. Soak the clothes in this borax-and-water solution until the mold is gone. Wash as usual. I find this better than bleach

for moldy shower curtains. Another way to attack mold is to add one cup of vinegar to the wash cycle.

- To eliminate static cling, add half a cup of white vinegar to the rinse cycle. To get rid of lint, add a quarter cup vinegar or lemon juice to the rinse cycle.
- My mom and grandmom made their own spray starch for ironing. Most commercial spray starch is loaded with chemicals, including silicon. If you want to do it the natural way, here is the recipe. Mix two to three teaspoons of cornstarch and one cup of warm water in a spray bottle. Shake well.
- This starch is for dark clothes only. (Make sure you mark the bottles "light starch" and "dark starch." When in a hurry one day, I confused the bottles and sprayed dark starch on a white blouse. I had to start from scratch and rewash the shirt.) To make starch for dark clothes, mix two to three teaspoons of cornstarch with half a cup of cooled black tea. Put the mixture in a spray bottle, and shake well.
- For an automotive-oil and grease-stain remover, use one liter of cola. For severe stains, soak overnight. Rinse and launder first thing the next morning. I have done this countless times for my husband and two sons. You cannot use a sink or bathtub to soak in this instance because the grease and dirt will clog the drains. I have a big plastic bucket just for this purpose.
- To make a popular homemade powdered laundry detergent, mix three cups (two bars) of Fels-Naptha or Zote soap, grated; one and a half cups of 20 Mule Team Borax; one and a half cups of Arm and Hammer washing soda; ten drops of lavender essential oil; and ten drops rosemary essential oil. (Or use the essential oils you prefer.) Mix the ingredients together in a large covered container and allow to stand for twenty-four hours before use. This allows the essential oils to permeate the detergent. Use one tablespoon per load for normal-sized loads. This will do about ninety loads of wash. Please remember to keep this mixture tightly covered and—as with all detergents—away from children.
- If you have hard water, combine twelve cups of borax, eight cups of baking soda, eight cups of washing soda, and eight cups of grated Fels-Naptha or Castile soap. Mix all of the ingredients well, and store in a tightly covered container. Use two tablespoons of the

powder per load. You may add essential oils if you like. Please make sure you finish all steps before you decide whether to add the oils. A lot of people are satisfied without them.

- For tough cleaning, combine two cups of grated Fels-Naptha soap, one cup of borax, one cup of washing soda, and one-third of a cup of OxiClean. Mix together, and use one or two tablespoons per load. Add essential oils if you like. Store covered; stir before each use.
- To make homemade liquid laundry detergent, you'll need one quart of boiling water, two cups of grated soap (Ivory, Fels-Naptha, or Zote), two cups of borax, and two cups of washing soda. Add the grated soap to the boiling water, and stir over low heat until all of the soap pieces are melted. Pour this solution into a large container and add the rest of the ingredients. Stir until everything is completely dissolved. Add two gallons of water, stirring well. Add essential oils at this point, if you like; I do not add them because this recipe gains such a fresh clean smell from the grated soap. The essential oils makes it too perfume-heavy. Cover, and let stand overnight. In the morning, the mixture will be a thin gel. Use one-fourth of a cup of the mixture per load. Be sure to stir it before each use. This mixture creates very low suds; it is excellent for HE washers.
- Here is another recipe for fabric softener; you'll need a quarter cup of baking soda and half a cup of white vinegar. Fill the washing machine with water. Add the baking soda, and then add the load of wash. During the final rinse cycle, add the vinegar; pour it into the fabric softener dispenser, if your machine has one. I tried adding all the ingredients together at the beginning, so I would not have to pay attention until the machine hit the rinse cycle. That did not work as well. This recipe is good for HE washers as well.

Go to my website, www.laundrywisdom.com, for updated suggestions and more recipes.

Mending Clothes

Mending is a simple chore, one that everyone should learn to do. It does not take a lot of expensive supplies to fix well-loved garments. Here are some easy instructions for sewing on a button and sewing a hem. Don't be afraid to do this. Follow the easy instructions below, and see for yourself.

How to Sew on a Button

If you don't have the button that fell off, check inside the garment for the extra button sometimes included by the manufacturers. When you buy new clothes, save any buttons attached to the tags. A small mailing envelope is a cheap and easy place to store buttons. A recycled can or container is another great idea. Make sure whatever you choose is rinsed out well and clearly marked. If you cannot find a button that matches, buy one that looks similar. I have a separate basket just for mending-related materials. I actually take the garment to the store, so I can match the buttons perfectly. Choose thread that either matches the fabric or is close to other thread used on the garment.

Cut a piece of thread about half a yard along, or as long as the distance from your fingertip to your elbow. Thread the needle through the eyehole. Fabric stores carry self-threading needles, which are great for teaching children and for those of us who cannot see well. They are not expensive and well worth it. After the thread is through the eyehole, move the needle slowly to the middle of the thread and fold the thread in half. Tie a knot so the end is secured. The thread is now doubled, and you are ready to sew. Place the button on top of the material at the place where you intend to sew it. Most of the time, you will be able to see where the last button was sewn on. A clever trick that my mom used was to place a toothpick or a match between the button and the material, so she would get the necessary slack. If you do not have either a toothpick or match, you can still continue; I have sewn hundreds of buttons without using either. Push the needle through the material from the underside and through one of the holes of the button. Pull all the way up until you feel the knot anchored against the cloth. Push the needle back down through the next hole on the button and through the material. Repeat the last two steps three more times, going up and down through the button hole and the material, so that each hole is secured by multiple strands. End with the needle on the material side, and secure it with one stitch into the fabric; then back out and knot. Take scissors, and cut the string above the knot. Bingo, you have just sewn on a button!

How to Sew a Hem

These are instructions for sewing a hem on a pair of slacks, but you can apply these rules to sewing a hem on anything—a dress or perhaps a skirt. One quick method to do this without sewing is called a Stitch Witchery. You can find it in any fabric store; and some supermarkets also carry it. It is a white tape that you place between the fabric, and iron it on. Follow the directions on the package. I have used it for years for quick fixes. I do not suggest using it on children's clothes. My boys went through many growing spurts, and I could put as many as four or five hems in one pair of jeans, as long as they did not destroy the knees too badly. When you use Stitch Witchery, it is permanent.

To sew a hem, you will need straight pins, tailor's chalk, scissors, a needle, and thread. Try on the pants, and decide on the desired length. Turn the pants inside out. Mark the desired length with tailor's chalk or pins. One note: sometimes, one leg is naturally shorter than the other. (The same is true of feet; one foot can be half a size smaller than the other.) Once you have pinned the hem in place, try the pants on again, very carefully, to make sure they are the desired length. Take off the pants, and lightly press the hemline in place. Trim off the excess fabric, leaving one and a half to two inches for dress slacks or two and a half inches for the pants of growing children. Press the new hemline well. Finish the raw edge of the fabric. Hand stitch or blind hem the fabric in place. Press well. Take care not to pull hand stitches too tight; you may create puckers in your fabric. Avoid making tucks in the hem by keeping the fabric flat as you sew. Always double-check the desired length before cutting the fabric.

CHAPTER EIGHT

THE JOY OF LAUNDRY

Never mistake knowledge for wisdom. One helps you make a living; the other helps you make a life.
—Sandra Carey

My aim in life is to learn what I can from my experiences, to act on that learning, and by my example to share what I have learned with others.
—Modern affirmation

The American Experience

For centuries, American women have completed their laundry despite extreme hardships—some with rocks, some with fire, some with wringers, and some with machines. I tip my hat to them all. The stories in this chapter are from real life, that wealth of experience that paints a picture of what wash day means to us all.

The Clothesline

© Marilyn K. Walker

A clothesline was a news forecast
To neighbors passing by.
There were no secrets you could keep
When clothes were hung to dry.

It also was a friendly link;
For neighbors always knew

If company had stopped on by
To spend a night or two.

For then you'd see the "fancy sheets"
And towels upon the line;
You'd see the "company tablecloths"
With intricate designs.

The line announced a baby's birth
From folks that lived inside,
As brand new infant clothes were hung,
So carefully with pride!

The ages of the children could
So readily be known;
By watching how the sizes changed,
You'd know how much they grown!

It also told when illness struck,
As extra sheets were hung;
Then nightclothes, and a bathrobe, too,
Haphazardly were strung.

It also said, "Gone on vacation now"
When lines hung limp and bare.
It told, "We're back!" when full lines sagged
With not an inch to spare!

New folks in town were scorned upon
If wash was dingy and gray,
As neighbors carefully raised their brows,
And looked the other way.

But clotheslines now are of the past,
For dryers make work much less.
Now what goes on inside a home
Is anybody's guess!

I really miss that way of life.
It was a friendly sign
When neighbors knew each other best
By what they hung on the line!

The Basic Rules for Clotheslines

By Lois Hermann

Here is a bit of nostalgia. You have to be a certain age to appreciate this.

1. Wash the clothesline before hanging any clothes; walk the entire lengths of each line with a damp cloth.
2. Hang the clothes in a certain order; always hang whites with whites, and hang them first.
3. Never hang a shirt by the shoulders; always by the tail. What will the neighbors think?
4. Wash day is Monday! Never hang clothes on the weekend, particularly on Sunday, for heaven's sake!
5. Hang the sheets and towels on the outside lines so you can hide your unmentionables in the middle (shielding them from perverts and busybodies, alike).
6. Hang the clothes even in sub-zero weather. The clothes will "freeze-dry."
7. Always gather the clothespins when taking down dry clothes. Pins left on the lines are tacky.
8. If you are efficient (thrifty), you will line the clothes up so that each item does not need two clothespins but shares one with the washed item next to it.
9. Take clothes off the line before dinner time, put them neatly folded in the wicker clothes basket, ready to be ironed.
10. Ironing? Well, that's a whole other subject!

Mom's Little Helper

By Joyce Murphy

This is a story my mom told me a long time ago. When she was young, her mother was not feeling well. My mother hung out the laundry; she was around five years old, so that would make it 1911. When her mother looked through the window to check on her, she was horrified at what she saw. Quickly, like it was an emergency, she straightened herself up and ran outside. She did not want to make my mother feel bad, but she just could not allow the laundry to be hung the way it was. She was so afraid the neighbors would see and think that she did it. She explained to my mother how to hang it correctly. All the shirts were hung together in a row, upside down with the pins on the seams, between the front and back panels. All the towels were hung together, never folded in half over the line, free of pins. That was a real no-no. Thank the good lord, she got to it before anyone else saw it!

Laundry Memory

By Bonnie Halko

My mother did not have a dryer when I was little, and she still washed most of the laundry by hand on a washboard in the basement in a huge deep laundry sink. Hanging laundry was done primarily according to the weather. Sunny days, cloudy days, any dry weather; temperature was never important, though I guess she did not hang clothes outside in super sub-zero degrees. I do remember laundry hanging in the basement, but rarely. The laundry hanging day is what I remember most fondly because my mother hung a low line just for me. I had my own pins, and I would hang everyone's socks, underwear, and, the most fun of all, doll clothes. I remember feeling extremely grown up and so important. I remember the excitement of a thunder storm popping up. Quick! Help get the laundry! The black sky was rumbling, and the white sheets were flapping like the sails on a ship. What an exciting race!

Laundry in Bristol, Pennsylvania

By Kate Grow

I grew up in a row home in Bristol, Pennsylvania. Hanging laundry was a religious ritual in my neighborhood. My dad, Foster, owned a company named Grow's Taxi, and I can remember he would drive me and my sister Tina around town in his cab. In those days, on a Monday you could literally see laundry for miles. If you had driven down the same streets the day before, however, you would not think you were at the same spot because not one person hung laundry on Sundays. I can remember looking at the different lines and admiring the different fashions of the times—beautiful dresses and scarves, blowing in the breeze. The one thing I can really remember is when a summer storm rolled in. We lived right by the Delaware River, and the storms would move in very quickly. All of the sudden, it was like someone opened the door to the chicken house; you would see women running in all directions, alerting their neighbors to get their wash down. In those days, it did not matter how well you knew your neighbor, you always addressed her by her last name when you were on the street. I can hear the shrieks. "Mrs. Black, hurry it is going to rain!" Then Mrs. Black would yell to her neighbor, "Mrs. Lorensky, hurry it is starting to rain!" It was absolutely amazing; in minutes, the streets would look like it was a Sunday—not a stitch of clothing in sight.

Mom's New-Fangled Clothes Pole

By Trudi Rosencrans

I grew up in Horsham, Pennsylvania. My parents had an old farmhouse on Jarrett Road. My mom was the first on the block to purchase a pole that had the clothesline connected to it. It worked like an umbrella; you pushed it up, and presto you had several lines. My dad had removed the old line, one single line that ran between two old poles. On one of the poles, he put a ball with a string attached—I think it was called a tether ball—that we would just punch around. Our neighbor, Mrs.

Edwards, who use to be a home-ec teacher, knew everything there was to know about housekeeping. She was first to see Mom's new clothesline; she said, "Joyce, where did you ever find that new-fangled gadget?" Soon the whole neighborhood was inquiring about the "new-fangled clothesline."

I am the youngest of five children, and my mom had lots of wash. My dad stood six feet, six inches tall, and my mom was five feet; she could never reach the old line. With her new line, she did not have to use additional poles to hold up the line in the center. My dad said the new pole was made in Australia, and they had a lot of snazzy ideas. Every Monday, my mom had all of the laundry hanging on that one line. Six sets of bed sheets and all of the whites for a week for seven people, all hanging no later than 8:15 AM. By lunch, the sheets were all down and folded neatly in a basket, ready to be ironed. One pole now held our family's entire wardrobe for the week. I can remember, right as rain, my mom ironing every piece of clothing she washed—underwear, sheets, every blessed thing we owned was ironed. The iron was set up in her bedroom, and I can see my mom standing there with the radio playing, ironing away. Once in a while you would hear her scream, "Oh, balls," which was cursing in those days; it meant that she'd found a stain she missed or a rip to mend. Everything was taken off the lines and ironed and put away. Each bed looked like a picture on the cover of a magazine, it was so perfect. Mom, did we ever thank you for all that work?

Big Stinky

By Lane McLeish

When I was a child, my family lived on what used to be a working farm, although they never worked it. Once the barn had burned down and the silo was sold, the 106-acre parcel was marked as an investment property, and my dad, being a realtor, thought he had found a worthy investment. My mother was not in complete agreement with his decision and frequently let him know that the isolation and crude amenities were definitely not suitable for a former city girl. By far, the worst of it had to be the cesspool, whose functioning diminished yearly and whose odor increased seasonally through the dog days of August. When the four of us went back to school in September, the system gradually recovered enough so that the ground firmed up as the muck receded back into the ground. My mother was the fresh-air and healthy-living icon in our family, preparing home-grown vegetables daily from our garden or freezer loading us up with vitamins throughout the winter. She enjoyed hanging her laundry in pleasant weather, but as our tolerance for the cesspool faded, the joy of fresh-smelling laundry did as well. Of course, the laundry lines ran straight across the area of the Big Stinky. After a few years of living on the farm, we were forbidden to play anywhere near that thing, and I would watch Mom from the safe distance of my swing set as she lugged the wet laundry up from the cellar and then tiptoed or leaped around the wet spots to hang everything. I longed to join her in the ritual as I had done for several years, handing up the soggy clothes as she clipped them to the lines with straight, wooden spring-loaded clothespins. These clothespins were considered quite the technological advancement as they didn't stretch out the fabric like the all wooden ones did. Eventually, she wearied of the task, which became a burden, and resorted to using the dryer for all but the sheets. When the Big Stinky ballet became too much of a chore, she contacted Blakeley Laundry of Trenton, whose staff would come down our quarter-mile-long unpaved road in all sorts of weather to pick up the week's dirty sheets, drawing them up in a big bundle with a double-bed top sheet as the sack. Then they'd deliver a neatly washed and pressed stack, wrapped up in brown paper in return, well worth the thirty-five cents per item.

Quite a few years later after graduating from college, I took the hippie version of the grand tour of Europe, spending a week or two in increasingly less touristy areas of the world. What started as a planned two-month excursion turned into a seven-month tour, ending with my last destination Essaouira, Morocco. Hundreds of hippies from dozens of countries came to call this seacoast town home in the winter of 1972; one of them was an enterprising guy named Michael from Newark, New Jersey, who made a living selling hash brownies to other hippies. I preferred mine as a breakfast treat, and after consuming one, I would walk along the old fort's parapets to find a quite spot to meditate for an hour or so while gazing across the Atlantic. My thoughts generally drifted back to my family and friends back home, but on two occasions I was transported to a place of bliss. One was a lotus garden in an unknown land of lush, green jungle, complete with sounds of chirping frogs and the scent of jasmine and lotus flowers. The other was what I could only describe as the space between two sheets hanging on a clothesline, flapping in the sweet wind.

True Story

By Beverly Phillips

I bought a new plastic shower-curtain liner. The cloying smell forced me to wash it on a speed cycle and then air it out on a clothesline. I neglected to bring it inside before dark. I also neglected to consider the season. Temperatures fell sharply overnight, and the wind chill increased to dangerous levels. I awakened to find the stark white curtain flapping madly in the wind, illuminated by rays of the rising sun. Only half of it remained. Millions of tiny, frozen, plastic shards had broken off and blanketed the lawn and my pristine garden beds. My husband and step-daughter saw the carnage and hightailed it off to work and school as fast as they could, knowing my blood-curdling screams would pierce the neighborhood as soon as I glanced out the kitchen window. For months afterward, as I worked in my vegetable beds and perennial patches, I found scraps of that $1.99 plastic shower-curtain liner.

Laundry Stories

By Cathryn Brownstein

Author's note: Here are three stories that were sent to me by Cathryn. I have included her original e-mail message because her writing is beautiful and well worth sharing. Let's all hope Cathryn Brownstein keeps on writing.

Dear Carin,
I would be honored to be included in your publication. I forwarded my stories and your reply to my mother, who urges me to take your

advice and enter the contest. I have no idea what to write about. I'm the kind of person who doesn't know I have created a great thing until I am halfway there. Every year I am expected to *make* a gift for my mother; no purchased items are accepted (unless they are secondhand like flea-market or thrift-shop treasures). Every year for her birthday, Christmas, and Mother's Day, I stress over what to make. Will it trump last year's? Will it fall short? Will she secretly hate yet graciously accept my procrastinated offering? Answer: it is perfect in my mother's eyes. The question will arise: is it wonderful only to her? No; everyone throughout my life has told me how creative I am. Maybe you are the person whose advice I will finally take.

By the way, while we were discussing the stories I wrote to you, my mother reminded me of the time she taught me to do the laundry. I overloaded the washing machine and flooded our apartment, causing water damage to the apartment below. I regret to inform you that I will not be telling you anymore about this story since I have conveniently forgotten the event.

But I will tell you that one day, as I was passing through the hallway, I heard a strange high pitched sound, not unlike the sound emitted by a smoke detector's dying battery. Assuming it was the latter, and of no concern to me, I went about my day. A few days later my mom mentioned having heard the same noise and, upon checking the assumed culprit, found the battery to be in full charge. Laundry day arrived; we swung the screeching metal, louvered doors aside, and the noise resumed. We checked the washing machine, which revealed no misplaced items. We checked the dryer, and a resonance of high pitches emanated from its cylindrical womb. We looked at each other and then peered back into the dryer, searching for the unseen thing that had created such a ruckus. Shrugging our shoulders at the now silent drum, we resumed our task. Over the swish of the rinse cycle, faint but robust chirping tickled our eardrums and seized our attention. We again investigated, to no conclusion, the source of the persisting announcement of existence. While we scrutinized the lack of visual clarification of this audible interference, the ever accurate washer ended its spin cycle, signaling a necessary transition of garments. The drum revolved continuously for two hours but delivered sopping garments. Faint chirping returned; our unsatisfied investigation, not to mention our still-drenched clothes, caused us to delve further into this mysterious connection. We took a deep breath, braced ourselves, and slowly dragged the malfunctioning contraption toward us.

I squeezed my child's body into the white-metal walled space and viewed the rear of the machine with concern. My mother climbed on top; I heard her gasp as the metal surface buckled under her knees. She shined a flashlight down, in the direction of the now-terrified chirping, directing me to unclamp the hose from the dryer. As I tugged on the tight nozzle, a flurry of vibration unnerved me, causing me to jump in response. This caused the nozzle to release and expel dust, emitting purple, pink, and grey fluffy pillows of lint as soft as cashmere. A small brown lump rolled out and lay unnoticed by my foot until I stood up to shake the hose. "Mom, it died." I picked it up in a folded piece of cashmere lint for her to review. Delighted chirping emanated from the unattached hose that I held in my left hand, giving relief to us that some survived the torrent of wasted heat forced on unsuspecting birds nesting in a convenient, warm and soft hole in the wall.

I handed the breathless fowl to my mother, who did not readily extend her hand, and evacuated the fluffy nesting materials. I pulled out a clump and felt something like a stick; removing the pinky soft encasing revealed a greenish paper stick. I almost added it to the trash pile until it slid between my fingers and slightly unfurled, exposing distressed yet familiar images. "Look what we got for our efforts!" I exclaimed as I handed my mother a $10 note. She smirked at me and climbed down off the dryer. I replaced the empty hose. We forced the metal cube into position and resumed the now possible task of drying our patient garments. As we passed through the living room to wash our hands in the kitchen, bird in hand, I looked out onto the porch and viewed my mother's leafy plants dancing in the breeze. We buried him in the prominent philodendron before making our way outside to discover how his family was able to obtain entrance to the dryer vent. A sizable ladder lent to us by the landscapers aided our reattachment of the duct cover, which was retrieved from its place in the bushes below. No more birds would face the same fate, at least not on our watch. We returned home to warm clothes and a quiet hallway, not to mention the $10, which bought us well-deserved ice cream cones. We ate while watching the philodendron dance in the breeze to the silent soul of a root-encased soul.

My mother always told me that clothes hung out in the cold during the winter dry beautifully crisp. This story is not about hanging out laundry, but rather about hanging it in. As a teenager, I stayed with a friend's family when my mother and I were not getting along. Not many of the people in my friend's household were employed, so needless to say, they didn't always pay their bills. The inevitable day came when certain utilities were turned off; mountains of laundry began to grow. They formed slowly at the foot of the beds and in the corners of the bathrooms. Dust settled like gray snow caps amid the heavy odor of long-forgotten garments. Out of season clothes were unearthed out of exigency.

The midday sun filtered in through dingy gray curtains and settled itself on the cool curves of a stately claw foot tub. The adornment of soft light gave presence to this vessel, which would become a transport to our few hours of productive play. Cold water flowed forcefully into the white porcelain canyon. Two young men and I rolled up our slacks to above our knees and stepped gingerly into the frothy surface. Rolled-up mounds of dust and cloth were submerged in the increasingly murky pool. The agitation cycle began as we braved the icy waters with numb limbs and spun the garments in the flurry of a mini conga line. Glistening bubbles sloshed on the slick tile floor, long since relieved of its necessary protective bath mat. The giggling conga dancers slipped and slid and grabbed at the bare curtain rod. The customary rinse cycle was skipped as we anticipated becoming human wringers in an attempt to re-create the spin cycle. I reached into the uncharted waters to retrieve a sopping manifestation of dye and cloth; my young friends gripped what we assumed were the corners and twisted. The commotion caused more sloshing bubbles to fly around, drenching our once-dry garments.

Weighed down with what else but water weight, we twisted the last few ropes of cloth over our heads in a celebration of completion as the streams of light slipped from our porcelain ship. We weary wringers clomped our unfeeling limbs onto the unforgiving tile deck. Dripping robes draped over our aching shoulders, we made our trek to the basement where contorted scraps of fabric would lie in darkness. A makeshift beam was our only aid in resurrecting these sad materials. Gentle breezes blew in the shadows from osculating window fans, which had been taken from their necessary posts in the heat-oppressed upstairs. The lingering soap caused corset-like qualities in our freshly washed garments. The deep wrinkles faded over time; apparel was lost, discarded, replaced, but lingering were the memories of our human washing machine.

This is a story from when I was much younger than in the above stories. I was at my beloved daycare; all the good little girls and boys were quietly coloring. I was pouring out buckets of worn-down crayons, their peeling paper covers dusted the table like waxy confetti. Gouged, naked crayons rumbled toward the cliff edge of our Formica snack/ activity table, threatening to disappear in the plush alphabet field below. Shushing glances were silently shot in my direction, followed closely by the disapproving deep breath sighs of our activities monitor. I started grappling the soon-to-be MIA culprits and barricaded them in a line by book-ending them with their former jailers. I started by lining them up in a rainbow pattern, several decent-length yellows and medium-sized oranges, some very mini reds, which led into skylines of blues and greens. All of a sudden I came upon an inmate without a category. In my hand, I held what I thought was the most unique crayon to have ever joined the ranks of the Crayola army; for resting in my cupped palm was a gold metallic nub. Barely an inch long, it peeked out at me, glistening as I peered at it through my clenched fingers. I faked a cough and slipped my treasure into the pocket of my new jeans. The rest of the day was a flurry of snacks, stories, and seesaw rides. I went home tired and fulfilled. A few days later, my pile of cute little laundry was swept away to be brightened. While intent on watching the TV, I was alarmed by my mother screaming in the hallway. I ran to her, and she held up several garments from the dryer that were spattered with a mysterious substance. I hid my face upon instant recognition of the metallic. My mother yelled the question, "What is this?" I couldn't bring myself to admit that I knew what the mystery substance was or how it had come to adhere itself to our clothes. My mother furiously began her fruitless efforts to scrape off the waxy shine. She finally abandoned her attempts and returned to drying the next load. While checking the dryness of the first load, she put her hand in pockets innocently checking for dampness but also for the usual lair of laundry murderers, i.e., tissues, pens, candies, and, low and behold, gold crayons! From that day on, I was expected to check every one of my pockets prior to laundry, especially dryer use, but she would secretly double-check. Gold crayons for everyone!—Cathyrn Brownstein, the Shakespeare of Laundry!

The Mystery of the Missing Socks

Carin Froehlich

We were the proud owners of an avocado Sears' dryer that ran for over twenty-six years with never one problem. Out of all of the appliances we ever had, that Sears' dryer should have been awarded the Old Faithful trophy. We were graced with the dryer by our sister and brother-in-law, Benny and Sarah. I believe it came with the purchase of their home years previously. My laundry was set up in an old farmhouse in the basement. I could care less that the colors of my washer and dryer were not the same, although many of my friends would comment, "How can you stand it?" What I could not stand was the basement.

Living in an old farmhouse is a way of life. You get used to the mice in the walls, the occasional bat flying around in the house, and all of God's other challenging little creatures that come to visit. The basement was a dark, damp, dingy place that came equipped with an etching engraved onto the stone walls. Four children's names and birth dates; on the top was the year 1896. When we bought the place I thought, how darling, they etched their children's names on the wall, sort of like how my mom used to line all of us children up, and write our heights from year to year on the wall. I can remember trying to sneak standing on my toes, or stretching my head so high. I always got caught. Years after we had moved into our farm house, I got talked into researching the history of the home. Big mistake! I found out all four children had died of the plague in the winter of 1896. They supposedly buried them in the basement because the grown was so frozen. Okay, that creeped me out. It did not matter if it was true or not; from that point on I flew down and back to do the laundry. There were always missing socks. I would find out that other families would suffer this misfortune. There was no way I was going to check for missing socks.

99

I was still seeking medical attention for the black snake I had seen wrapped around the plumbing. My husband got such a kick out of my horror. The old farmers, including my father-in-law, Sonny, said, "Don't you know having a snake in your basement is a good thing? They'll eat all your rodents. What are you, a city girl?" Let me tell you, the city was looking pretty good to me!

One winter day I noticed a very strange odor; thinking a mouse had died in the walls, a common event, and the snake wasn't doing his job, I went on with life. Another week passed, as I was grabbing the clothes from the dryer, the clothes had rather a rancid odor. When my husband came home from work, I pushed him down the basement to investigate. Of course, I immediately sprinted up the steps. I heard him banging and fiddling around, and then an "I'll be damned." Oh, what could it be this time? Up he came with what seemed a sad look on his face. It was my daughter's hamster. Gobbler had gotten out of his cage, for the one hundredth and last time. The cause of the odor in the dryer killed Old Faithful. The socks, some in excellent condition, had gotten behind the drum; others were trying to escape through the dryer vent. Gobbler and Old Faithful had a proper burial, and now I know the secret of the missing socks!

Clothesline Harmony or the Wedding Catcher

By Anonymous

The woman who told me this story told me I could not use her name. She was worried her sister-in-law would find out, and she would get in a lot of trouble for repeating the story. I will change her name to Stella. This story starts in a small town in the early 1960s. Stella was from a large family: four brothers and three sisters. In those days, everyone hung their clothes outside when weather was permissible and in the basement when the weather was harsh. Stella's mother was an excellent housekeeper. She took great pride in keeping an organized home. One of Stella's best friends, Barbara, had a horrible crush on Stella's brother Tommy. No matter what those girls tried, Tommy would not pay an inch of attention to Barbara.

As the years went on, Barbara lost her braces and became a very attractive young lady, and Tommy would punch you in the arm if you called him "Tommy." He became Tom. Barbara lived two doors down from Stella. Every time they passed Barbara's house, she would be out hanging the wash in perfect order. Stella's mother would just marvel at how Barbara hung her wash. She would yell at her own daughters, "Why can't you girls get in to the knack of hanging laundry just like Barbara? Look at what a beautiful job Barbara does." Barbara's own mother had no idea what had gotten into her daughter, who was always begging to hang the laundry although she was secretly the messiest child ever. Barbara's mother just couldn't figure it out. The seasons changed, and the girls grew up, and Tom asked Barbara to marry him. Stella's mom was beside herself with happiness. "I finally will have a clean-nick in my family," she said. One month after Tom and Barbara's wedding, Stella claims, all of the sudden Barbara's wash looked like hell hanging on the line. She just would throw it across the line without pins and other offenses that kept the neighborhood gossip at a record high. Barbara laughingly told Stella, "Honey, I could give a rat's ass about laundry. I only did it years ago so your mother would like me. I told you I was going to marry your brother!" Stella's mother never spoke about Barbara's laundry act again.

Camping Laundry

by Sally Whiteson

My favorite memory from when we were children was a vacation day. We had a Scamper camper, and our family was heading to California. We were camping at a Kampgrounds of America (KOA) outside of Kansas City. There were tornado warnings on the radio, but my father said that it was hogwash. He proceeded to set up camp, and Mother went and did the laundry. Mother washed everything we had packed and hung it out to dry. The sky suddenly got a funny green-black color. There it was in the horizon—a real tornado. My parents were well-bred people from the East and had no idea what to do. My mother was screaming at the top of her lungs, "Kids, get to the bathrooms!" I could not have thought of a worse place to go. We all huddled in the women's bathroom as the tornado came through. I could see through the slats the trees touching the ground and heard a noise that sounded like we were in front of a train. When it was over, we peeked outside and saw a different world. Our Scamper stood on all four wheels but with tree limbs broken all over it. That day, Father named the camper "Betsy"; she was a good girl. We could not find our laundry at first; it was finally discovered at the top of an old pine. Firemen came to the camp to check on the campers. My mother asked one fireman if he could get a ladder to retrieve her laundry. The fireman laughed at my mother and told her, "Honey, God is the only person that has a ladder that tall. Be grateful you are all alive and move on." Father hitched "Betsy" to the car, and we drove straight back home to Philadelphia. We had only the clothes on our backs and no shoes. I remember that as my favorite vacation ever. As the years went on, Father and Mother would laugh till they cried, telling the story of Old Betsy and the tornado.

Grandma's Queenie 2 Trip

By Barbra Williams

My grandma spoke for two years about her plans to sail on the "Queenie," i.e., the *Queen Elizabeth 2*, also known as the QE2. She took in laundry to make the extra money she needed to take the trip. This was all my grandma could talk about; it was her goal, her dream, her savings.

Grandma set sail on April 10, 1962. We took her to the dock. I had never seen such a ship in my life. There were hundreds of people waving good-bye from the balconies. Mom said she could see grandma. All I saw was ant-like people waving the hell away.

We got a postcard from Grandma a few weeks later with a picture of the QE2. Grandma stated she was right under the smoke stack in the picture. Years later, I found out that when she boarded the ship she was placed right above the laundry room. Noisy and steamy, twenty-four hours a day, but Grandma was thrilled she had made it this far. Her next postcard stated that she got to sit at the captain's table for dinner. They had overbooked the ship's passages and that is why my grandma ended up in a room by the laundry. The captain was so grateful my grandma did not complain that he actually invited her to dine at his table many times over the course of the trip. My mother said it could not have worked out any better. Whenever I look at a picture of the QE2, I look for the smoke stack, and I see Grandma waving away.

Laundromat, New York City, 1968

By Annie Percichello

The Laundromat was a place in which women enjoyed each other's company immensely. Mr. Santiago was the Laundromat's second-generation owner. He used to shuffle around with his son and fix the machines. His wife had a little office in the back where you would go to get change or the keys to the bathroom. When a stranger stopped in at the Laundromat, all the joy was sucked out of the building. The women would then whisper to each other.

They all had their political views but shared them only at the Laundromat. I can remember that Daddy was a strict Republican and so was Mama. Once at the Laundromat, Mama's views drastically changed. Mama sat next to Daddy every Sunday at church. Come Monday at the Laundromat, Mama would read and discuss books on all types of religions. The women had a place in the office where they kept all that reading material. Mama listened only to Daddy's music at home. At the Laundromat, she would turn up the transistor radio, and they would all do the Twist around the machines. I remember Mama telling me how she loved Joni Mitchell, but we never listened to Joni at home. Mama cooked all of Daddy's favorite meals; at the Laundromat, Mama's mouth would water over exotic recipes that she would copy down. She never made them.

I can remember Mama excusing herself from her chores on Saturdays so she could do some extra wash at the Laundromat. Daddy had to fix his own lunch, and he did not like it. Mama and her friends were always down there to help their friends through divorces or whatever; these women, as close as they were on Mondays, never came or called to our home. Mama said, "Daddy would disapprove of that."

The Laundromat was a woman's space. I grew up and went off to college. My parents got a divorce. I knew my Mama was just fine because she had the women at the Laundromat. I sent her an 8-track player with an 8-track tape of Joni Mitchell. It was the perfect gift.

Wash Day

By Lidia Welks

The smell of clean sheets, fresh from the sun and wind, is the best smell in the world. From the time I was a small child until my adult years, no matter where I have traveled or what continent I have lived on, the wash always has that sweet smelling fragrance. I believe it is a gift from Mother Nature. No manufacturer or wizard can ever duplicate the fragrance.

I can remember doing laundry with my grandmother on the farm in Delaware. I tried to explain this wonderful event to my children. They rolled their eyes and said, "Mother, you had no car, or TV. How did you ever exist?" I get the same reply from my grandchildren today. Perhaps you would be interested to hear?

We had one huge tub for washing and a twin tub for rinsing. Every Saturday evening, my grandmother would start boiling water for the wash tub. Once it was filled, we would all get a bath. Yes, in the same bath water. Grandma then would take the dirty dark clothes and soak them in the dirty bath water. In the other tub, her whites would soak till Monday. You had to get up at the crack of dawn in order to get the job done. The water would be boiled on the wood stove, and the old wringer would be hauled off the porch and filled with hot water.

First the white sheets and white garments; into the wash tub they went. I can still hear that swooshing sound, back and forth for about fifteen minutes. Then off to the cold-water rinse and a dip in this bluing solution to keep things white. Then it was time for the final rinse. The light-colored dresses and aprons followed. We all took turns cranking the wheel on the washer to wring the clothes dry. Off to the line. God help you if those sheets touched the ground. No matter what the season was, winter or summer, we followed the same protocol. I can remember on horrible winter days, the snow would be so high grandma would haul the entire ensemble to the basement and hang the clothes to dry. The whole house would be filled with the smell of fresh wash.

The finest of moments was "girl" talk. There was no other time it was allowed except for wash day. Grandma and my aunts would talk about a lot of things. I learned a lot about life at those Monday clotheslines.

I think about this a lot now that I am in my nineties. After the war [World War II], my husband, Harold, came home, and the first thing we bought was a house. I was pregnant with our second child; the second thing Harold bought was a washer. No dryer, but I did not want one any way.

Our daughter Jane was born shortly after the washer was installed. My grandma and mother came to visit and help. They spent most of their darn time by that washer. Just standing there not saying a word, sighing. They just could not get over how much time it saved. The years went on, and I had four more children. I had that same Whirlpool washer until Harold passed away He was always handy in the home; he could fix anything. The professionals would come in, take a look, and have no idea what Harold had done. They could not figure out his repairs, one way or another. My washer took its last ride on a beautiful summer day in June.

My children all grew up and moved in many directions. Carol, our youngest, went back to our native Holland. To this day, Carol is the only one of children who does laundry the way I taught them. The other five are out buying new washers and dryers every other year, it seems. They do not hang their clothes out to dry. They claim that they just don't have the time. I have to understand, they say, that they hold full-time employment, and that they must use a dryer. Full-time employment; when I think of those words it really gets my goat. What the hell did they think we spent our days on the farm doing? We worked harder than they did in a day, than they did at their fancy desk jobs in a month.

I know. I had a desk job shortly after Harold died. I worked forty hours a week. I had to change my laundry habits; there was no more Monday wash. I had to hang some weeks on a Sunday. No one in my neighborhood seemed to mind. These children today are so busy doing nothing. My friends and I think that it is from watching too much television. That darn contraption is forever telling you that "you have no time." My children listen to that all the time. You know, they have televisions in just about every room. I am telling you the truth. My grandchildren are worse yet. They take all of their laundry to a place, and the people do it for them. If my mama could see this, she'd be so disappointed. I could cry, thinking back to those laundry days; they were always happy days. I learned so many lessons about life working the wash. Today, they don't have the privilege of learning the good life. They are always telling their children "Go out and play," or they are driving their children any where they want to go. Those children have no responsibilities; they have no chores. Every time those brats come to visit me, they want nothing to do with knowing me. All they can do is play with a blinking game in their overfed paws. Elsie down the hall tells me that her grandchildren do the same. Elsie says, all she hears is how well this one and that one is doing in school, like that is all they have to life. Anna tells me, all she hears is how excellent her grandchildren are in sports. They just don't get the fact that they are raising lazy people. You know that the good life has nothing to do with how much money you have. The good life is learning and appreciating the free life nature offers you, that good feeling in your soul. Do you know what I mean?

Author's note: "Wash Day" was told to me by Lidia Welks. She died a few weeks after telling me this story, She died in her sleep on freshly laundered sheets that I'd washed for her the previous day. I went to many nursing homes to retrieve laundry stories. To my great surprise, I met amazing people with whom I only wish I could have spent more time. When I selected their stories, I offered to do their sheets and hang them on my clothesline. I ended up feeling quite sad for the rest of them and offered to do their pillow cases. Every Monday, I have clotheslines filled with pillow cases. On Tuesdays, I drop them off at the nursing homes. This is my way of giving back to my community. Shortly after Lidia passed away, I got a wonderful letter from her family. They thanked me for my time and patience with their mother, and best of all, they now have found the time to occasionally hang their laundry. Lidia once asked me if I knew what she meant about that feeling in your soul. I wish you could hear me Lidia; I know exactly what you mean.

A Note to the Reader

I am currently writing another book, this time about housekeeping. Please e-mail any stories or cleaning tips that you would like to submit to: laundrypals@comcast.net or pleasecook@msn.com.

Mail written letters to:
Laundry Wisdom
PO Box 246
Bedminster PA 18910

Please visit www.laundrywisdom.com for updated information and a complete list of laundry-product sources mentioned in this book.

Finally, I'd like you to think of *Laundry Wisdom* as your book as well as mine. Please use the blank pages that follow to keep track of your own laundry solutions or stories, and send me a note when you find something that works.

Wishing you fresh air, sunshine, and success,

Carin Froehlich

MY STORY

Notes

Notes

Notes

Notes

Notes

Notes

Notes

Made in the USA
Las Vegas, NV
20 November 2023

81218578R00072